M000267014

Aunt Phil's Trunk Volume Three

Teacher Guide

Bringing Alaska's history alive!

By
Laurel Downing Bill

Special credit and much appreciation to Nicole Cruz for her diligent efforts to create the best student workbook and teacher guide available for Alaska history studies.

Aunt Phil's Trunk LLC, Anchorage, Alaska
www.auntphilstrunk.com

International Standard Book Number 978-1-940479-29-3
Printed and bound in the United States of America.

First Printing 2017
First Printing Second Edition 2017
First Printing Third Edition 2018

Photo credits on the front cover, from top left: Native shaman with totem, Alaska State Library, Case and Draper Collection, ASL-P-39-782; Eskimo boy, Alaska State Library, Skinner Foundation, ASL-P44-11-002; Prospector, Alaska State Library, Skinner Foundation, ASL-P44-03-15; Athabascan woman, Anchorage Museum of History and Art, Crary–Henderson Collection, AMHA-b62-1-571; Gold miners, Alaska State Library, Harry T.Becker Collection, ASL-P67-052; Chilkoot Pass, Alaska State Library, Eric A. Hegg Collection, ASL-P124-04; Seal hunter, Alaska State Library, George A. Parks Collection, ASL-P240-210; Women mending boat, Alaska State Library, Rev. Samuel Spriggs Collection, ASL-P320-60; Teacher photo, Alaska State Library, J. Simpson MacKinnon Photo Collection, ASL-P14-073.

Table of Contents

TABLE OF CONTENTS

Welcome to *Aunt Phil's Trunk Volume Three* Teacher Guide!

Read the chapters associated with each Unit. Then complete the lessons for that Unit to get a better understanding of Alaska's people and the events that helped shape Alaska's future.

I hope you enjoy your journey into Alaska's past from the years 1912 to 1935.

Laurel Downing Bill, author

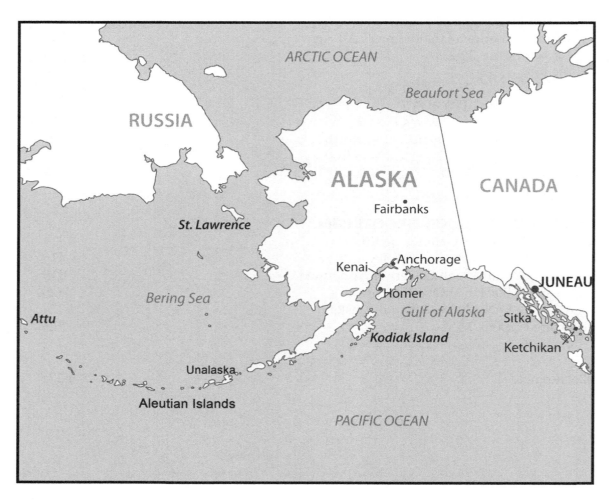

Instructions for using the Aunt Phil's Trunk
Alaska History Curriculum

The *Aunt Phil's Trunk* Alaska History Curriculum is designed to be used in grades 4-8. High school students can use this curriculum, also, by taking advantage of the essay and enrichment activities throughout the book. The next few pages give further instruction on how to use this curriculum with middle school students, high school students and in classroom settings.

This curriculum can be taught in multiple grade levels by having your older students complete all reading, study guide work and enrichment activities independently. Students of all grade levels can participate in daily oral review by playing games like Jeopardy or Around the World.

This curriculum was developed so that students not only learn about Alaska's past, but they will have fun in the process. After every few lessons, they can test their knowledge through word scramble, word search and crossword puzzles.

Notes for parents with younger students:

Enrichment Activities occasionally direct your child to watch educational videos on YouTube.com or link to other Websites to learn more about the topic that they are reading about in the lesson. You may want to supervise younger children while they are using the Internet to be sure that they do not click on any inappropriate content. This also provides a good opportunity to discuss Internet safety with your child/children.

How to use this workbook at home

Aunt Phil's Trunk Alaska History Curriculum is designed to be used in grades 4-8. High school students can use this curriculum, also, by taking advantage of the essay and enrichment activities throughout the book. The next page gives further instruction on how to use this curriculum with high school students.

This curriculum can be taught in multiple grade levels by having your older students complete all reading, study guide work and enrichment activities independently. Students of all grade levels can participate in daily oral review by playing games like Jeopardy or Around the World.

For Middle School Students:

1. **Facts to Know:** Read this section in the study guide with your student(s) before reading the chapter to get familiar with new terms that they will encounter in the reading.

2. **Read the chapter:** Read one chapter aloud to your student(s) or have them read it aloud to you. Older students may want to read independently.

3. **Comprehension Questions:** Younger students may answer the comprehension questions orally or write down their answers in the study guide. Use these questions to test your student(s) comprehension of the chapter. Older students should answer all questions in written form.

4. **Discussion Questions:** Have your student(s) answer these questions in a few sentences orally. Come up with follow-up questions to test your student(s) understanding of the material. Older students may answer discussion questions in written essay form.

5. **Map Work:** Some chapters will contain a map activity for your student(s) to learn more about the geography of the region that they are learning about.

6. **Enrichment and Online References:** (Optional) Assign enrichment activities as you see fit. Many of the online references are from the Alaska Humanities Forum website (http://www.akhistorycourse.org). We highly recommend this website for additional information, project ideas, etc.

7. **Unit Review:** At the end of a unit, your student will complete Unit Review questions and word puzzles in the study guide. Students should review all the chapters in the unit before completing the review. Parents may want to assist younger students with the word puzzles.

8. **Unit Test:** (Optional) There is an optional test that you can administer to your student(s) after they have completed all the unit work.

How to use this workbook for high school

1. **Facts to Know:** Your student(s) should read this section in the study guide before reading the chapter to get familiar with new terms that they will encounter.

2. **Read the chapter:** Your student(s) can read aloud or independently.

3. **Comprehension Questions:** Use these questions to test your student(s) comprehension of the chapter. Have your high schoolers write out their answers in complete sentences.

4. **Discussion Questions:** Have your student(s) answer these questions in a few sentences orally or write out their answer in essay form.

5. **Map Work:** Some chapters will contain a map activity for your student(s) to learn more about the geography of the region that they are learning about.

6. **Enrichment and Online References:** Once your high schooler has completed all the reading and study guide material for the chapter, assign additional reading from the enrichment material using the online links or book lists. Encourage your student(s) to explore topics of interest to them.

Many of the online references are from the Alaska Humanities Forum website. We highly recommend this website for additional information, project ideas, etc.

7. **Unit Review:** At the end of a unit, your student will complete Unit Review questions and word puzzles in their study guide. Students should review all the chapters in the unit before completing the review.

8. **Unit Test:** (Optional) There is an optional test that you can administer to your student(s) after they have completed all the unit work.

9. **Oral Presentation:** (Optional) Assign a 5-minute oral presentation on any topic in the reading. Encourage your student(s) to utilize the additional books and online resources to supplement the information in the textbook. Set aside a classroom day for your student(s) to share their presentations.

10. **Historical Inquiry Project:** Your student(s) will choose a topic from the reading to learn more about and explore that topic through library visits, museum trips, visiting historical sites, etc.

Visit https://www.nhd.org/how-enter-contest for detailed information on how to put together a historical inquiry project. You may even want to have your students enter the national contest.

How to use this workbook in the classroom

Aunt Phil's Trunk Alaska History Curriculum was created for homeschooling families, but it also can work well in a co-op or classroom setting. Here are some suggestions on how to use this curriculum in a classroom setting. Use what works best for your classroom.

1. **Facts to Know:** The teacher introduces students to the Facts to Know to familiarize the students with terms that they will encounter in the chapter.

2. **Read the chapter:** The teacher can read the chapter aloud while the students follow along in the book. Students also may take turns reading aloud.

3. **Comprehension Questions:** The teacher uses these questions to test the students' comprehension of the chapter. Students should write out the answers in their study guide and the teacher can review the answers with the students in class.

4. **Discussion Questions:** The teacher chooses a few students to answer these questions orally during class. Alternatively, teachers can assign these questions to be completed in essay form individually and answers can be shared during class.

5. **Map Work:** Some chapters will contain a map activity for your students to learn more about the geography of the region that they are learning about. Have your students complete the activity independently.

6. **Enrichment and Online References:** Assign enrichment activities as you see fit.

7. **Daily Review:** Students should review the material for the current unit daily. You can do this by asking review questions orally. Playing review games like Jeopardy or Around the World is a fun way to get your students excited about the material.

8. **Unit Review:** At the end of a unit, your student will complete Unit Review questions and word puzzles in the study guide. Have students review all the unit chapters before completing.

9. **Unit Test:** (Optional) There is an optional test that you can administer to your students after they have completed all the unit work.

10. **Oral Presentation:** (Optional) Assign a 5-minute oral presentation on any topic in the reading. Encourage your students to utilize the additional books and online resources to supplement the information in the textbook. Set aside a classroom day for students to share their presentations.

11. **Historical Inquiry Project:** Your student(s) will choose a topic from the reading to learn more about and explore that topic through library visits, museum trips, visiting historical sites, etc.

Visit https://www.nhd.org/how-enter-contest for detailed information on how to put together a historical inquiry project. You may even want to have your students enter the national contest.

How to grade the assignments

Our rubric grids are designed to make it easy for you to grade your students' essays, oral presentations and enrichment activities. Encourage your students to look at the rubric grid before completing an assignment as a reminder of what an exemplary assignment should include.

You can mark grades for review questions, essay tests and extra credit assignments on the last page of each unit in the student workbook. Use these pages as a tool to help your students track their progress and improve their assignment grades.

Unit Review Questions

Students are given one point for each correct review and fill-in-the-blank question. Mark these points on the last page of each unit in the student workbook.

Essay Test Questions

Students will complete two or more essay questions at the end of each unit. These questions are designed to test your students' knowledge about the key topics of each unit. You can give a student up to 20 points for each essay.

Students are graded on a scale of 1-5 in four categories:

1) Understanding the topic
2) Answering all questions completely and accurately
3) Neatness and organization
4) Grammar, spelling and punctuation

Use the essay rubric grid on page 11 as a guide to give up to 5 points in each category for every essay. Mark these points for each essay on the last page of each Unit Review in the student workbook.

Word Puzzles

Word puzzles that appear at the end of the Unit Reviews count for 3 points, or you can give partial points if the student does not fill in the puzzle completely. Mark these points under the extra category on the last page of each Unit Review in the student workbook.

Enrichment Activities

Most lessons contain an enrichment activity for further research and interaction with the information in the lesson. You can make these optional or assign every activity as part of the lesson. You can use the provided rubric on page 12 to give up to 5 points for each assignment. Mark these points under the extra category on the last page of each Unit Review in the student workbook.

Oral Presentations

You have the option of assigning oral presentations on any topic from the unit as extra credit. If you choose to assign oral presentations, you can use the provided rubric to grade your student on content and presentation skills. Discuss what presentation skills you will be grading your student on before each presentation day.

Some examples of presentation skills you can grade on include:

- Eye contact with the audience
- Proper speaking volume
- Using correct posture
- Speaking clearly

Use the oral presentation rubric grid on page 12 as a guide to give up to 10 points. Mark these points under the extra category on the last page of each Unit Review in the student workbook.

Rubric for Essay Questions

	Beginning 1	Needs Improvement 2	Acceptable 3	Accomplished 4	Exemplary 5
Demonstrates Understanding of the topic	Student's work shows incomplete understanding of the topic	Student's work shows slight understanding of the topic	Student's work shows a basic understanding of the topic	Student's work shows complete understanding of the topic	Student's work demonstrates strong insight about the topic
Answered questions completely and accurately	Student's work did not address all of the questions	Student answered all of the questions with some accuracy	Student answered all questions with close to 100% accuracy	Student answered all questions with 100% accuracy	Student goes beyond the questions to demonstrate knowledge of the topic
Essay is neat and well organized	Student's work is sloppy and unorganized	Student's work is somewhat neat and organized	Student's essay is neat and somewhat organized	Student's work is well organized and neat	Student demonstrates extra care in organizing the essay and making it neat
Essay contains good grammar and spelling	Student's work is poorly written and hard to understand	Student's work contains some grammar, spelling and punctuation mistakes, but not enough to impede understanding	Student's work contains only 1 or 2 grammar, spelling or punctuation errors	Student's work contains no grammar, spelling or punctuation errors	Student's work is extremely well-written

11

Rubric for Oral Presentations

	Beginning 1	Needs Improvement 2	Acceptable 3	Accomplished 4	Exemplary 5
Preparation	Student did not prepare for the presentation	Student was somewhat prepared for the presentation	Student was prepared for the presentation and addressed the topic	Student was well-prepared for the presentation and addressed important points about the topic	Student prepared an excellent presentation that exhibited creativity and originality
Presentation Skills	Student demonstrated poor presentation skills (no eye contact, low volume, appears disinterested in the topic)	Student made some effort to demonstrate presentation skills (eye contact, spoke clearly, engaged audience, etc.)	Student demonstrated acceptable presentation skills (eye contact, spoke clearly, engaged audience, etc.)	Student demonstrated good presentation skills (eye contact, spoke clearly, engaged audience, etc.)	Student demonstrated strong presentation skills (eye contact, spoke clearly, engaged audience, etc.)

Rubric for Enrichment Activities

	Beginning 1	Needs Improvement 2	Acceptable 3	Accomplished 4	Exemplary 5
	Student's work is incomplete or inaccurate	Student's work is complete and somewhat inaccurate	Student completed the assignment with accuracy	Student's work is accurate, complete, neat and well-organized	Student demonstrates exceptional creativity or originality

UNIT 1: EARLY COOK INLET

LESSON 1: COOK INLET TIMELINE

FACTS TO KNOW

Cook Inlet – Area of southcentral Alaska that stretches 180 miles from the Gulf of Alaska to Anchorage

Dena'ina – Native people of the Cook Inlet area (also called Tanaina)

Alaska Homestead Law – Provided land for settlers in Alaska

COMPREHENSION QUESTIONS

1) When was the earliest-known human habitation of the Cook Inlet area? What people group lived there? What people group displaced them?
Based on anthropological data from the Beluga Point area near Anchorage, the earliest-known human habitation of the Cook Inlet area was by Eskimo people about 3000 B.C. Athabaskan Dena'ina Indians (also called Tanaina) entered Cook Inlet through mountain passes to the west as early as 500 A.D. and as late as 1650 A.D., displacing the Eskimos. (Page 9)

2) How did the Cook Inlet receive its name?
Captain James Cook did not name the inlet – instead he called it "River Turnagain." British Lord Sandwich later ordered that it be called "Cook's River." Explorer George Vancouver changed "River" to "Inlet" in 1792. (Page 10)

3) Why did the Dena'ina population in the upper inlet plummet by half between 1835-1845? *The Russians brought smallpox and tuberculosis. The population of the Dena'ina in the upper inlet plummeted to 816 by 1845, half of what the Russians had counted when they'd arrived 10 years earlier. (Page 12)*

4) Due to mounting diplomatic problems in Europe and Asia, the _Russians_ sold Alaska to the _United States_ for $7.2 million in 1867. When _Alexander King_ discovered gold around _Kenai_ in 1888 and _Resurrection Creek_ in 1893, thousands of hopeful _miners_ streamed into Cook Inlet.

5) What was the purpose of the Alaska Homestead Law in 1898? What revisions were made in 1903 and 1912?
Congress extended homesteading to Alaska under the Alaska Homestead Law in 1898. The homesteader was limited to 80 acres and limited entry to surveyed land. The amendment in

13

1903 expanded the acreage to a maximum of 320 acres. The act again was revised in 1912, when Congress passed the Three Year Homestead Law. It reduced the length of residence required, specified the amount of land to be cultivated and changed the requirements for absences from the property. (Page 16)

6) Congress passed the *Territorial Organic Act of 1912* that made Alaska a U. S. territory.

DISCUSSION QUESTION

(Discuss this question with your teacher or write your answer in essay form below. Use additional paper if necessary.)

Briefly summarize the history of Cook Inlet from early human habitation to 1914.

_____
_____
_____
_____
_____
_____
_____
_____
_____
_____
_____
_____
_____
_____
_____
_____
_____
_____

ENRICHMENT ACTIVITY

Using Chapter 1, create a Cook Inlet timeline of events. Begin with the first wave of early human habitation in the inlet, and then end with the 1914 Alaska Railroad Act.

LEARN MORE

The Cook Inlet Collection: Two Hundred Years of Selected Alaskan History, Morgan Sherwood. Anchorage: Alaska Northwest Publishing Company, 1974.

UNIT 1: EARLY COOK INLET

LESSON 2: RAILROAD MAKES HEADLINES

FACTS TO KNOW

Seward – A city in the Kenai Peninsula named for U.S. Secretary of State William H. Seward

John Ballaine – Founder of the city of Seward who believed the town would be the metropolis of a great territory

Alaska Railroad Act – Allowed the president to locate, construct and operate a railroad that would unite the Pacific Ocean with the navigable waters of Interior Alaska

COMPREHENSION QUESTIONS

1) What newspaper headline "resurrected" the town of Seward? Why was this news so important to the residents of Seward?

Congress had authorized construction of an Alaska railroad, and the Seward newspaper's headline proclaimed that its little port city would become the terminus for the project. That was welcome news to the residents of Seward, who had seen two railroads go bust in the past decade – railroads that had offered the promise of delivering Alaska's rich resources to tidewater and jobs to those in the picturesque little town in Prince William Sound. (Pages 18-19)

2) How did this news change the economy of Seward?

Houses, which the owners may have given away earlier in the day, were selling at boom prices by the afternoon. Speculators swallowed up choice lots. New stores opened and stores already there worked feverishly to expand and enlarge. Building went on around the clock. Boatloads of people came to Seward to work on the railroad. (Page 19)

3) What obstacles delayed the building of the railroad? What happened to John Ballaine's Alaska Central Railroad company?

Due to rough terrain, lack of capital and closure of coalfields by the federal government in 1906, his Alaska Central Railroad went bankrupt in 1908. It reorganized as the Alaska Northern in 1910. At no time was the railroad even able to earn out-of-pocket expenses. Its "tracks, bridges and docks were not adequately maintained, and by 1914 it was hardly in operating condition" (Page 22)

4) How did Judge James Wickersham play a part in getting the railroad built?
By 1912, Judge James Wickersham, then Alaska's delegate to Congress, urged both houses to pass legislation enabling the government to build a railroad in Alaska along a route to be determined by the president. President Woodrow Wilson signed the Alaska Railroad Act into law in 1914. (Page 22)

5) Why did the government eventually change their plans to make the railroad headquarters in Seward? What area was chosen as the headquarters?
As land prices in Seward ballooned and Ship Creek's central location to the entire project became more evident, officials decided to move operations from Seward. The reason for the change, officials said, was because the government was confronted with legal obstructions and high prices in its purchase of the Alaska Northern and surrounding property. (Page 23)

DISCUSSION QUESTION

(Discuss this question with your teacher or write your answer in essay form below. Use additional paper if necessary.)

What do you think about the poem by Pat P. Cotter on Pages 24 and 25?

_____
_____
_____
_____
_____
_____
_____
_____
_____
_____
_____
_____

ENRICHMENT ACTIVITY

Learn more about the Alaska railroad route by visiting https://www.alaskarailroad.com/ride-a-train/route-map
See how many cities you recognize from your lesson on the route map.

LEARN MORE

Read more about Alaska railroad construction by visiting http://www.akhistorycourse.org/southcentral-alaska/1915-1930-the-railroad-years

UNIT 1: EARLY COOK INLET

LESSON 3: KNIK WITHERS

FACTS TO KNOW

Knik – Small trading town in Cook Inlet
Alaska Engineering Commission – A group of three men (William C. Edes, Lt. Frederick Mears and Thomas Riggs) were appointed to scout out the railway route

COMPREHENSION QUESTIONS

1) What industry did Knik rely upon beginning in 1834?
The people of Knik first started trading with white men when the Russians established a mission there in 1834. The Russians converted the Dena'ina Indians to Christianity and began trading with them and through them with the Indians of Interior Alaska. (Pages 26-27)

2) How did activities in other parts of Alaska bring life into the settlement of Knik? (Hint: gold rush and Iditarod Trail)
Gold found in the Interior in 1903 brought prospectors and supplies to Knik, where they then disembarked and headed north. Construction of the Iditarod Trail brought mail bound for Nome, and shipments of gold by dog team came back down the trail to meet boats at Knik. (Page 27)

3) What event caused Knik to become the major trading center for gold and coal?
Gold was found in the Talkeetna Mountains to the north and coal discovered in the Matanuska Valley. Knik soon became the major trading center for the gold and coal mines, as well as the supplier for various sawmills in the Matanuska Valley, Susitna River Basin and Willow mining area. (Pages 27-28)

4) How did the Alaska Railroad Act of 1914 cause Knik to become a ghost town?
The route chosen to connect Seward to the Matanuska coalfields and on to Fairbanks bypassed the community on Knik Arm, and its residents eventually moved to either Wasilla or the railroad camp on Ship Creek that became Anchorage. Knik became a ghost town. (Page 29)

DISCUSSION QUESTION

(Discuss this question with your teacher or write your answer in essay form below. Use additional paper if necessary.)

Why were the residents of Knik angry at the government?

_____
_____
_____
_____
_____
_____
_____
_____
_____
_____
_____
_____
_____
_____
_____
_____
_____
_____

LEARN MORE

Read more about the ups and downs of the building of the Alaska railroad by visiting http://www.akhistorycourse.org/americas-territory/alaskas-heritage/chapter-4-11-railroad-transportation

TIME TO REVIEW

Review Chapters 1-3 of your book before moving on to the Unit Review. See how many questions you can answer without looking at your book.

Early Cook Inlet Landmarks
Word Search Puzzle Key
Find the words listed below

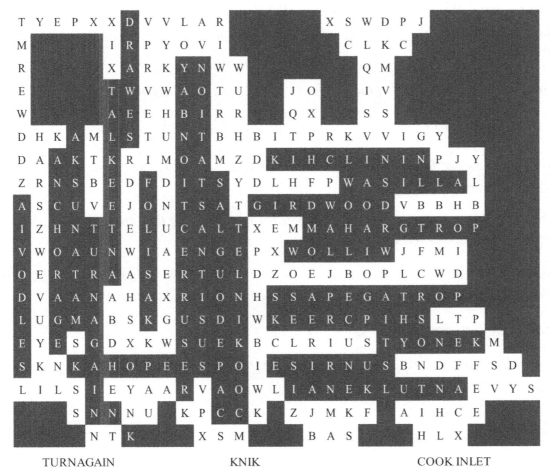

TURNAGAIN	KNIK	COOK INLET
KASILOF	KENAI	TYONEK
SELDOVIA	NINILCHIK	EKLUTNA
PORT GRAHAM	SUSITNA STATION	PORTAGE PASS
CAPE DOUGLAS	TALKEETNA	MATANUSKA
WASILLA	ANCHORAGE	SHIP CREEK
SUNRISE	HOPE	GIRDWOOD
SEWARD	RESURRECTION BAY	WILLOW

UNIT 1: EARLY COOK INLET

REVIEW LESSONS 1-3

Write down what you remember about:

Cook Inlet – _Area of southcentral Alaska that stretches 180 miles from the Gulf of Alaska to Anchorage_

Dena'ina – _Native people of the Cook Inlet area, also called Tanaina_

Alaska Homestead Law – _Provided land for settlers in Alaska_

Seward – _A city in the Kenai Peninsula named for U.S. Secretary of State William H. Seward_

John Ballaine – _Founder of the city of Seward who believed the town would be the metropolis of a great territory_

Alaska Railroad Act – _Allowed the president to locate, construct and operate a railroad that would unite the Pacific Ocean with the navigable waters of Interior Alaska_

Knik – _Small trading town in Cook Inlet_

George W. Palmer – _Opened a store called Palmer's Cache after America's purchase of Alaska_

Fill in the blanks:

1) _Athabascan Dena'ina Indians_ entered Cook Inlet through mountain passes to the west as early as _500 A.D._ and as late as 1650 A.D., displacing the _Eskimos_. The _Dena'ina_, also called _Tanaina_, adapted the Alutiiq peoples' knowledge of living in a coastal region, such as using _kayaks_ for saltwater fishing, and subsisted entirely on the _fisheries and wildlife._

2) When _Alexander King_ discovered gold around _Kenai_ in 1888 and _Resurrection_ Creek in 1893, thousands of hopeful miners streamed into Cook Inlet. Stampeders, who had to travel to _St. Michael_ or _Skagway_ to get to the rich diggings in the Yukon, began demanding an all-American route be blazed. After many years of surveying routes, the government deemed that _a railroad_ would be a good mode of transportation.

3) Congress extended homesteading to Alaska under the _Alaska Homestead_ Law in _1898_. It differed from the original provisions of the 1862 law, which covered the rest of the _United States_, in that a homesteader was limited to _80 acres_ and limited entry to surveyed land.

4) 'EXTRA! EXTRA!' An extra in a small town like _Seward_ is a sensation, but more sensational was the news. The U. S. government had chosen _Seward_ as the saltwater _terminus_ for its proposed government _railroad_.

5) Boatloads of men arrived from the states seeking work on the new _railroad_, which was to be built from the deepwater port of _Seward_ to Alaska's _Interior,_ where abundant resources like _coal_ and _gold_ awaited transportation to the coast.

6) President _Woodrow Wilson_ signed the _Alaska Railroad Act_ into law in 1914 and Secretary of Interior Franklin Lane appointed three men, geologist _Thomas Riggs_ and experienced railroad builders _William C. Edes_ and _Lt. Frederick Mears_, to the Alaska Engineering Commission.

7) Residents of _Seward_ weren't happy when the _railroad headquarters_ was established at _Ship Creek (which became Anchorage)_ instead of their town. The reason for the change, officials said, was because the government was confronted with legal obstructions and _high prices_ in its purchase of the Alaska Northern railroad and surrounding property.

8) The residents of *Knik*, which had become a thriving *supply* center during the late 1890s, first started trading with white men when the *Russians* established a mission there in 1834.

9) After the American purchase of Alaska, *George W. Palmer* opened a store there in the 1880s called *Palmer's Cache*. It relied upon the local *fur trade.*

10) The *Alaska Railroad Act* of 1914 spelled the end of Knik. The route chosen to connect *Seward* to the Matanuska coalfields and on to *Fairbanks* bypassed the community on *Knik* Arm, and its residents eventually moved to either *Wasilla* or the railroad camp on Ship Creek called *Anchorage*.

Alaska Central Railway, seen above in 1906, was the first railroad going out of Seward. By 1908 it had gone bankrupt. Next came Alaska Northern, seen below in 1910. Alaska Northern became part of the Alaska Railroad in 1914.

23

UNIT 1: EARLY COOK INLET

UNIT TEST

Choose *two* of the following questions to answer in paragraph form. Use as much detail as possible to completely answer the question.

1) Describe three important events that occurred in the timeline of Cook Inlet history from 3000 B.C. to 1914. Why were these events important?

2) What sleepy town received good news in the summer of 1914? What good news did this town receive? In what ways did this news immediately impact the town? How did the government ultimately let down this town?

3) What industries did the town of Knik rely upon beginning in 1834? How did the Alaska Railroad Act affect the town of Knik?

_____
_____
_____
_____
_____
_____
_____
_____
_____
_____
_____
_____
_____
_____
_____
_____
_____
_____
_____
_____
_____

TEACHER NOTES ABOUT THIS UNIT

UNIT 2: EARLY RAILROAD DAYS

LESSON 4: RAILROAD BIRTHS ANCHORAGE

FACTS TO KNOW

Anchorage – Cook Inlet city that was chosen as the headquarters of the Alaska Railroad

Woodrow Wilson – U.S. president who pushed to build the Alaska Railroad in 1914

COMPREHENSION QUESTIONS

1) The *Alaska Railroad Act* authorized the president to locate, construct and operate a railroad that would unite the *Pacific Ocean* with the navigable waters of *Interior Alaska*. The railroad could not exceed *1,000* miles in length and could not cost more than *$35 million*.

2) Why did President Woodrow Wilson create the Alaska Railroad Commission? Who did he appoint to this group?
Wilson appointed William C. Edes, a renowned locating engineer, as chairman, as well as Frederick Mears, who'd been the chief engineer on the Panama Railroad relocation project. The third member, Thomas Riggs, had broad experience in Alaska as a geologist, mining engineer and surveyor. Their job was to scout out railway routes. (Pages 30-31)

3) What two routes did the Alaska Railroad Commission study?
The team studied two primary routes: The Cordova-based route that had been examined earlier by the 1912 Alaska Railroad Commission, and the "Susitna Route," which was basically aligned like the present Seward to Fairbanks route. It also checked out auxiliary links, including Portage Bay to Turnagain Arm and a branch to the Matanuska Valley. (Page 32)

4) Which route was chosen after the commission completed their study?
Within a week of the commission's report, Alaska's Gov. John Franklin Alexander Strong wrote a friend: "I am unofficially advised that work will begin this spring on a line between Ship Creek in Cook Inlet to the Matanuska coal fields." (Page 32)

5) According to a 1921 report to the Secretary of Interior, how much did it cost per mile to build the railroad? What supplies were needed to build the railroad? From where did the supplies come?

It cost about $80,240 per mile, including terminals, to build the railroad, the report said. Ocean docks, building materials and supplies of every description had to be transported 1,500 miles from Seattle, the nearest Pacific Coast port. (Page 33)

DISCUSSION QUESTION

(Discuss this question with your teacher or write your answer in essay form below. Use additional paper if necessary.)

Describe some of the challenges that residents of early Anchorage faced.

_____
_____
_____
_____
_____
_____
_____
_____
_____
_____
_____
_____
_____
_____
_____
_____
_____
_____

LEARN MORE

Read more about the reconnaissance survey for the Alaska railroad by visiting http://content.lib.washington.edu/alaskawcanadaweb/kuskokwim.html

MAP ACTIVITY

The Alaska Railroad Commission studied two routes to Alaska's Interior– one from Cordova and one from Seward – before choosing the Susitna route. Fill in the boxes for places that sit along those routes: 1) Cordova 2) Childs Glacier 3) Seward 4) Portage/Whittier 5) Anchorage 6) Wasilla 7)Talkeetna 8) Denali 9) Fairbanks

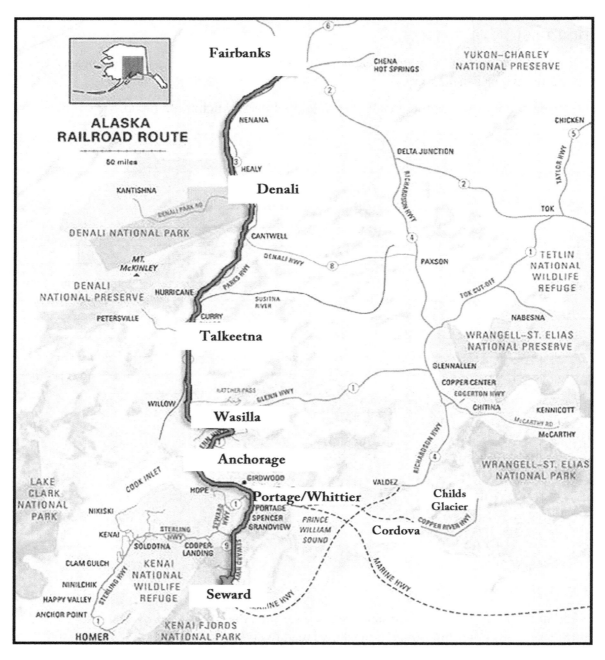

UNIT 2: EARLY RAILROAD DAYS

LESSON 5: SHIP CREEK BLOSSOMS

FACTS TO KNOW

Ship Creek – A creek located between Seward and Fairbanks
Lot auction – Process of buying and selling a lot of land going to the highest bidder
World War I – Global war originating in Europe that lasted from 1914 to 1918

COMPREHENSION QUESTIONS

1) Why did the Alaska Engineering Commission recommend Ship Creek as the headquarters for the government railroad?
While studying routes to get those resources to tidewater, the Alaska Engineering Commission came upon Ship Creek, which was centrally located between Seward and Fairbanks. It had a protected anchorage that could be dredged and a large amount of flat land on which a construction camp could be built. (Page 36)

2) How did George C. Hazelet describe Ship Creek to the *Cordova Daily Times* in 1915?
Hazelet said it was the largest town he ever saw. "From 2,000 to 2,500 people are fed, housed, and their wants, in a way, taken care of in tents, all located on the government railway terminal ground." He saw many lodging houses, restaurants, grocery stores, two drug stores, one sawmill, one picture show, one newspaper and other small businesses. "There are 600 to 700 men out of work." He observed contention between the people and the government. (Pages 36-39)

3) What were living conditions like in the early days at Ship Creek?
Living conditions were less than ideal as more and more job seekers arrived along the creek. With no sewers, and Cook Inlet tides providing the only means of waste disposal, the Alaska Engineering Commission surgeon warned that the new settlement's water supply soon would become contaminated. (Pages 39-40)

4) What were the results of the first town lot auction in Ship Creek in July 1915?
The first land auction on July 10 opened with enthusiastic bidding. At its conclusion, the Land Office had auctioned 655 lots for about $150,000. Local merchants had paid more for lots along Fourth Avenue than anywhere else in town. Those first bids on Fourth Avenue property averaged $548 per lot, whereas the average price for other townsite lots ran about $225. Corner lots along the center of the avenue, between C and F streets, sold for between $800-$1,000, twice the appraised value. (Page 43)

5) How did the area known as Ship Creek receive the name Anchorage?
It's widely believed that Anchorage, submitted by Ray McDonald, won in an election held on Aug. 2, 1915. But according to Alaska Engineering Commission records discovered by M. Diane Brenner, past archivist for the Anchorage Museum of History and Art, the vote went to Alaska City. However, the settlers later learned that the U.S. Post Office had already arbitrarily named the new Alaska settlement Anchorage. (Page 50)

6) Describe the first public school in Anchorage.
Completed in November 1915, the public school was constructed to serve about 90 students. From the beginning, residents labeled the school "entirely inadequate," "unsanitary" and "of an order of the early eighteenth century." The school lacked a solid foundation, paint and a satisfactory heating system, and its unheated outdoor toilets didn't meet townsite standards. One teacher taught 70 primary students in half-day shifts. (Pages 52-54)

7) What important historical event caused the Alaska Railroad workforce to go from more than 5,600 to 2,800 by 1918? Why?
World War I pulled many railroad workers away from Anchorage. President Woodrow Wilson recognized that the United States could be drawn into the war at any moment by the act of some obscure German submarine commander. The resulting preparedness boom drew unskilled labor away from the Alaska Railroad project. (Page 58)

DISCUSSION QUESTION

(Discuss this question with your teacher or write your answer in essay form below. Use additional paper if necessary.)

How did the government railroad lead to the development of a new city called Anchorage?

_____

_____

_____

ENRICHMENT ACTIVITY

Imagine that you are one of the thousands of people that traveled to Ship Creek in order to work on the railroad. Write a letter to your friend back home about your adventure. What is the town like? What are your living conditions like? What is the work like?

LEARN MORE

Watch this short YouTube video about the building of the Alaska Railroad:
https://www.youtube.com/watch?v=c5U9o3E-XLI

UNIT 2: EARLY RAILROAD DAYS

LESSON 6: GOLDEN SPIKE MYSTERY

FACTS TO KNOW

Railroad spike – Large nails used to hold the rails in place

Warren G. Harding – The first U.S. president to visit Alaska

Metlakatla – First stop on U.S Predient Warren G. Harding's trip to Alaska where he was welcomed by Tsimshian people with traditional music and dancing

Ketchikan – Southeast Alaska city that greeted President Harding and his party with a brass band

COMPREHENSION QUESTIONS

1) When was the railroad completed? What was done to commemorate the occasion?
The railroad was completed in July 1923. To commemorate the end of the 470-plus-mile project, President Harding traveled to Alaska to drive in the last spike. (Page 66)

2) According to Secretary of Commerce Herbert C. Hoover, how did President Warren Harding feel about traveling to Alaska in 1923?
Hoover later said Harding was thrilled about coming to Alaska and his enthusiasm was like that of "a school boy entering on a holiday," according to Warren G. Harding by John W. Dean. Harding spent hours on the deck of the U.S. transport Henderson watching in awe as the ship swept past the territory's majestic landscapes. (Page 67)

3) What did President Harding do on July 15, 1923, to complete the construction of the Alaska railroad?
President Warren G. Harding drove a golden spike into the rail in Nenana to complete the construction of the railroad. (Page 70)

4) What did President Harding say about Alaska when he reached Seattle? How did he become ill at the end of his trip?
"Alaska is designed for ultimate statehood," he said. "In a very few years we can well set off the Panhandle and a large block of the connecting Southeastern part as a state. The region now easily contains 90 percent of the white population and of the developed resources." Two days out of Sitka, Harding began experiencing severe abdominal pain after eating crab drenched in butter. (Pages 71-72)

5) President Warren Harding died on Aug. 2, 1923, less than three weeks after he drove the golden spike into the last piece of track for the Alaska Railroad. What are some theories about his cause of death?

For years some people claimed the president had been murdered by his wife for his unfaithfulness. Other theories surrounding Harding's demise suggested members of his cabinet killed the President to keep him from investigating their wrongdoings, while others said he committed suicide because he'd learned his friends were crooks and he was weighed down by their bad deeds. Physician's records revealed that he had a heart attack. (Pages 72-74)

DISCUSSION QUESTION

(Discuss this question with your teacher or write your answer in essay form below. Use additional paper if necessary.)

Explain the mystery of the golden spike.

_____
_____
_____
_____
_____
_____
_____
_____
_____
_____
_____
_____
_____
_____
_____
_____
_____
_____

LEARN MORE

Read more about the 29th U.S. president by visiting https://www.whitehouse.gov/1600/presidents/warrenharding

TIME TO REVIEW

Review Chapters 4-6 of your book before moving on the Unit Review. See how many questions you can answer without looking at your book.

Many Alaska children were excited to see U.S. President Warren G. Harding in July 1923, the first president to visit Alaska.

Alaska Railroad

Crossword Puzzle

Read Across and Down clues and fill in blank boxes that match numbers on the clues

Across

3 Goods transported in railroad cars
5 This was a huge problem on dirt streets along Ship Creek in 1915
6 Alaska Engineering Commission overlooked this in the new town along Ship Creek
11 Pacific Coast port where building materials and supplies began journey to build Alaska Railroad
12 Railroad started in 1902 & went bankrupt 1908
15 Type of engine that powered Alaska Railroad trains in early 1900s
19 Route chosen to lay tracks for the Alaska Railroad
21 Area just north of Ship Creek that had mining and grazing potential
23 Supply center whose Indian name means "fire"
26 Name of last car in a railroad train
29 Name for person who labors building a railroad
31 Superintendent of lot sales in Ship Creek
34 Name of deep-water bay at Seward
35 Fourth Avenue of Anchorage was laid out for this purpose

Across (Continued)

36 Name of railroad that took over Seward's railroad in 1910
39 Structure used to carry railroad across a river or other obstacle
41 This sprang up on the north bank of Ship Creek when 2,000 people arrived in 1915
43 A continuous line of rails for a railroad
46 First, Second and Third avenues of Anchorage were set aside for this purpose
47 Name of second school that opened in Anchorage in December 1917
48 First car that provides power to pull the trail
49 U.S. president who pounded last spike in Alaska Railroad to signify its completion 1923
52 A large nail that secures railway rails to the ties
53 A yellow ore found abundantly in Alaska that needed to be transported to Seward
55 Valley just north of Ship Creek that had potential to develop into a farming community
56 Ship that carried Lt. Frederick Mears to Alaska in late April 1915

Down

1 Secretary of Interior in 1914
2 U.S. President who signed the Alaska Railroad Act in 1914
4 Geologist for Alaska Railroad
7 The building of the railroad
8 Name for what became Anchorage that actually won the most votes during an election on Aug. 2, 1915
9 Member of the Alaska Engineering Commission
10 Town chosen as the end of the Alaska Railroad
13 Commission created in 1914 to build Alaska Railroad
14 The farthest point reached in constructing a railroad
16 Man who wanted to name town after Secretary of State William H. Seward

(Down Continued)

17 An extensive area containing a number of coal deposits
18 Author of the "Wandering Boy"
20 The area of land alongside a coast
21 Judge who urged Congress to pass legislation to build an Alaska railroad
22 Major event that pulled workers away from building the Alaska Railroad in 1918
24 Country from which much of the machinery used to build the Alaska Railroad originated
25 The first cabin on Ship Creek was built by this man
27 Name of U. S. transport that brought a U.S. president to Alaska in 1923
28 Man who wrote the poem "The Unholy Trinity"
30 A structure extending alongshore or out from the shore into a body of water

Alaska Railroad

Crossword Puzzle Key

(Down Continued)

32 Member of the Alaska Engineering Commission

33 First butcher in Anchorage

37 Started one of the first dry goods businesses in Anchorage

38 Alaska's Territorial governor at the time that the Alaska Railroad began construction

42 Indians who had fish sites and smokehouses around Ship Creek in 1914

44 The chimney of a locomotive

45 Headquarters for the U.S. government's railroad project

50 Spacing of rails on a railway track

51 Term for end point of Alaska Railroad

54 Name of railroad car that has special comfort and sleeping berths

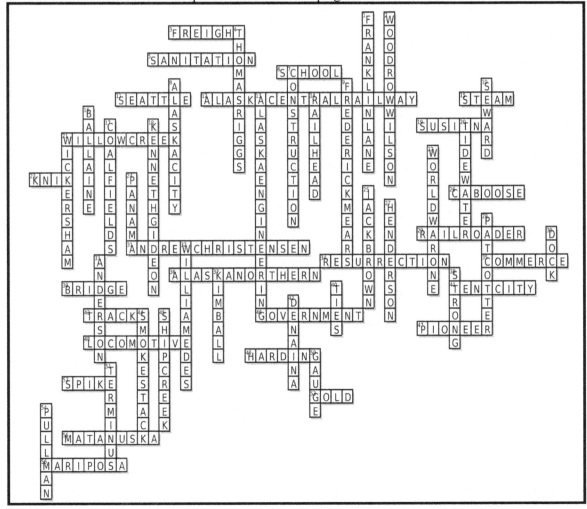

UNIT 2: EARLY RAILROAD DAYS

REVIEW LESSONS 4-6

Write down what you remember about:

Anchorage – *Cook Inlet city that was chosen as the headquarters of the Alaska Railroad*

President Woodrow Wilson – *U.S. president who pushed for the Alaska Railroad*

Ship Creek – *A creek located between Seward and Fairbanks*

Lot auction – *Process of buying and selling a lot of land going to the highest bidder*

World War I – *Global war originating in Europe that lasted from 1914 to 1918*

Railroad spike – *Large nails used to hold the rails in place*

President Warren G. Harding – *The first U.S. president to visit Alaska*

Metlakatla – *First stop on U.S President Warren G. Harding's trip to Alaska where he was welcomed by Tsimshian people with traditional music and dancing*

Ketchikan – *Southeast Alaska city that greeted President Harding and his party with a brass band*

Fill in the blanks:

1) At first the _Alaska Engineering Commission_, which was created in 1914 and developed the railroad, only saw the site at _Ship Creek_ as a major construction camp and terminal point along a route to link Seward with Interior Alaska.

2) Ship Creek's central location to the entire _railway_, and skyrocketing land prices in the deepwater port of _Seward_, caused the commission to change its mind in 1915 and make _Ship Creek/Anchorage_ its headquarters.

3) While studying routes, the _Alaska Engineering Commission_ came upon _Ship Creek_, which was centrally located between _Seward_ and _Fairbanks_. It had a protected _anchorage_ that could be dredged and a large amount of _flat land_ on which a construction camp could be built.

4) Upon hearing of the new construction camp in Cook Inlet, hoards of men and women poured into _Ship Creek_ hoping to snag jobs building _Alaska's railroad_. When Frederick Mears stepped off the steamer _Mariposa_ in late April 1915, he saw hundreds of _tents_ and _temporary shelters_ housing those awaiting work.

5) One observer gave the _Cordova Daily Times_ an account of what he saw on a trip to the _railroad_ camp. "I found the largest _tent town_ I ever saw," George C. Hazelet said in an interview on June 29, 1915. "From 2,000 to 2,500 people are fed, housed, and their wants, in a way, taken care of in _tents_, all located on the government _railway terminal_ ground."

6) Living conditions were less than ideal as more and more _job seekers_ arrived along the creek. With no _sewers_, and Cook Inlet tides providing the only means of _waste disposal_, the Alaska Engineering Commission surgeon warned that the new settlement's _water supply_ soon would become contaminated.

7) The first _land auction_ on July 10, 1915, opened with enthusiastic bidding. At its conclusion, the _Land_ Office had auctioned _655 lots_ for about _$150,000_. Local merchants had paid more for _lots_ along _Fourth_ Avenue than anywhere else in town.

8) The _U.S. Post_ Office arbitrarily named the new Alaska settlement at Ship Creek _Anchorage_.

9) To commemorate the end of construction on the Alaska Railroad, _U.S. President Warren G. Harding_ traveled to Alaska to _drive in the last spike_. He was the first _U.S. president_ to visit the territory.

10) President _Warren G. Harding_ hammered a symbolic _golden spike_ into the railroad track at _Nenana_ on _July 15, 1923._ The $600 _golden spike_ then was replaced with an _iron_ one to finish the track.

11) President Harding began experiencing _severe abdominal pain_ after eating crab drenched in butter. _Tainted shellfish_ was suspected. The President became more ill as he traveled by train to San Francisco. Harding, 57, _died_ on Aug. 2, less than three weeks after he _drove the golden spike_ into the last piece of track for the _Alaska Railroad_.

Possible Names for Ship Creek Town in Forest
Word Search Puzzle Key
Find the words listed below

MATANUSKA	TERMINAL	NEW KNIK
ALASKA CITY	SHIP CREEK	WOODROW CITY
GATEWAY	WINALASKA	HOMESTEAD
LANE	WHITNEY	BROWNSVILLE
ANCHORAGE		

UNIT 2: EARLY RAILROAD DAYS

UNIT TEST

Choose *two* of the following questions to answer in paragraph form. Use as much detail as possible to completely answer the question.

1) Why did the Alaska Engineering Commission choose Ship Creek as the Alaska Railroad headquarters? How did this choice impact the city?

2) Describe the early days of Anchorage. How did the city get its name? What were the living conditions like? What caused the railroad workforce in Anchorage to be cut by almost half in 1918?

3) When was the Alaska railroad completed? What was done to commemorate the occasion? What mystery surrounded this ceremony?

_____
_____
_____
_____
_____
_____
_____
_____
_____
_____
_____
_____
_____
_____
_____
_____
_____
_____
_____
_____
_____
_____
_____
_____

TEACHER NOTES ABOUT THIS UNIT

UNIT 3: BIG CITY CONCERNS

LESSON 7: VOTERS CHOOSE SELF-RULE
LESSON 8: FIRST MAYOR TACKLES VICE

Note: Read both chapters 7 and 8 before completing this lesson.

FACTS TO KNOW

Petition – A formal written request typically signed by many people

Judge Frederick Brown – Judge of the Third Judicial Division in Valdez who granted Anchorage residents their first local election

Mayor Leopold David – The first mayor of Anchorage

Prohibition – A ban on production, transportation and sale of alcoholic beverages

COMPREHENSION QUESTIONS

1) Why did a group of Anchorage citizens file a petition with the U.S. District Court at Valdez in 1920? What did the petition say?
While many of its residents seemed content to have the Alaska Engineering Commission continue to govern the day to day affairs, others thought it was time the citizens took over management of the town. The petition requested that a special election be held to determine the wish of the majority in the former tent city. (Page 74)

2) What were the results of the election ordered by Judge Frederick Brown? What ruling did Judge Brown make after the election?
The election returns showed a count of 328 votes for incorporation and 130 votes against. Another 85 blank ballots had been stuffed into the ballot box. After careful consideration, Judge Brown ruled the 85 blank votes were to be ignored. He decided it was as if those voters had not been to the polls at all and that Anchorage had voted itself into incorporation. (Page 75)

3) What was Mayor Leopold David's primary responsibility when he was elected in 1920? What laws did he put into place?
When Judge Leopold David became Anchorage's mayor, he helped the new city council develop ordinances to provide law and order. They included establishing a 9 p.m. to 5 a.m. curfew for youth younger than 16, setting a speed limit of 8 mph in town and outlawing spitting in public places. He instituted the curtain ordinance to try to curtail gambling. (Pages 78-80)

4) What were some of the issues that Mayor David faced as the new mayor? Why was bootlegging a problem in Alaska in the early 1900s?

Some of the issues that he faced in Anchorage were gambling, bootlegging and prosititution. Bootlegging was difficult to regulate because it provided a revenue stream for many of Anchorage's citizens. (Pages 80-83)

DISCUSSION QUESTION

(Discuss this question with your teacher or write your answer in essay form below. Use additional paper if necessary.)

Why do you think the people of Anchorage wanted to elect their leaders? How was this different than having the Alaska Railroad Commission govern their day to day affairs?

_____
_____
_____
_____
_____
_____
_____
_____
_____
_____
_____
_____
_____
_____
_____
_____
_____

ENRICHMENT ACTIVITY

Write a letter to a local politician. You can write about a problem that you see in your community, something you would like to see in your neighborhood or simply a letter of encouragement.

Use this Website link for more ideas and information on how to find the right person to send your letter to: https://www.education.com/magazine/article/How_Write_Letter_Politician/

LEARN MORE

Read more about early Anchorage history by visiting http://www.cookinlethistory.org/anchorage-history.html

UNIT 3: BIG CITY CONCERNS

LESSON 9: FIRST POLICE CHIEF MURDERED

FACTS TO KNOW

Anchorage City Council – Elected city government leaders in Anchorage
John "Jack" Sturgus – The first chief of police in Anchorage
Vice – Immoral and criminal activities

COMPREHENSION QUESTIONS

1) According to author Kenneth Gideon, how did bootleggers work around Anchorage's prohibition laws in the early 1900s?
Liquor came in over the trail, on hand sleds and by dog team during the winter. In the summer when navigation opened up it might be found in five-gallon cans inside bales of hay. Cases of canned tomatoes would prove other than tomatoes. (Page 84)

2) What important issue did the Anchorage City Council ask Chief Sturgus to focus on?
The police and jail committee reported that there were several complaints made in regard to open gambling in pool rooms, cigar stores and other places in town. The council instructed the chief of police to rigidly enforce the provisions of the ordinance relative to gambling. (Pages 86-87)

3) What happened to John Sturgus within a few weeks of working as police chief?
Chief of Police John "Jack" Sturgus was gunned down in an alley off E Street in 1921. (Page 87)

4) Describe some of the theories people had about what happened to John Sturgus.
One suggested the chief was killed "while endeavoring to make an arrest or while watching in the rear of the drugstore for some man under suspicion." Other theories suggested that Sturgus had been "murdered by members of an illicit liquor gang," "in revenge" because of the "activity of the marshal's office during the past week." The Alaska Dispatch also suggested Sturgus' death was connected to Anchorage's thriving illegal bootlegging business when it reported that the chief may have been killed in revenge for the "capture of 12 moonshine outfits last week by United States marshals." (Page 89)

DISCUSSION QUESTION

(Discuss this question with your teacher or write your answer in essay form below. Use additional paper if necessary.)

How would you approach the vice problems that Anchorage had when John Sturgus was hired? Would you do things differently? Explain how you would have handled the problems.

_____
_____
_____
_____
_____
_____
_____
_____
_____
_____
_____
_____
_____
_____
_____
_____
_____
_____

ENRICHMENT ACTIVITY

Law enforcement has the very difficult job of protecting and serving our communities. Take some time to get to know more about your local police department by either visiting its Website or visit your local police station in person. If you decide to visit in person, prepare two or three questions to bring with you.

LEARN MORE

Read more about the history of police in the United States and other parts of the world by visiting https://www.britannica.com/topic/police

UNIT 4: A FEW CITY FOREFATHERS

LESSON 10: PIONEER PHILANTHROPIST ARRIVES

FACTS TO KNOW

Zachariah J. Loussac – One of Anchorage's first philanthropists
Philanthropist – A person who seeks to help others, often by being generous with money

COMPREHENSION QUESTIONS

1) What led Z.J. Loussac to travel from New York to Alaska?
Since the streets of New York weren't paved with gold, as so many immigrants had been led to believe, Loussac decided to go where he thought he could pick up gold by the handful. (Page 90)

2) What happened the first two times that Loussac attempted to make it to Alaska?
His first attempts to reach the Klondike gold fields landed him broke in Great Falls, Montana, where he had to work as a drugstore clerk until he could save enough money to return to New York. On his second attempt, he made it to Seattle. It took him three months to get on a boat to Nome, where he failed at prospecting. He started a drugstore, which he lost to fire and then again when prospectors began leaving the area to chase gold in Ruby. (Pages 91-92)

3) How did Loussac advertise his drugstore in Anchorage? What did he offer in his drugstore?
Loussac advertised his drugstore as having "what you want when you want it." Loussac put in a writing desk and supplied it with paper and envelopes free to anyone who wanted to write a letter. He offered a phonograph with all the latest records, and customers were invited to play them without charge. He imported fresh flowers for customers. (Pages 92-93)

4) How did Loussac describe the amount of money that he made during World War II?
The mushroom growth of Anchorage during World War II was the turning point for his business. Not only was he able to pay off all his debts, but he found money "rolling in by the bushel baskets!" (Page 93)

46

5) What gift was hailed as the "most generous gesture ever made by a living Alaskan toward his fellow Alaskans"?

Loussac wanted to do something for Anchorage – the city had been so good to him – and decided to give it half his wealth. His gift was hailed as the "most generous gesture ever made by a living Alaskan toward his fellow Alaskans." (Pages 95-96)

6) What did Loussac say was the best thing that happened to him in Anchorage?

Loussac claimed that the "greatest thing that has happened to me here (in Anchorage) was that here is where I met my wife." (Page 97)

DISCUSSION QUESTION

(Discuss this question with your teacher or write your answer in essay form below. Use additional paper if necessary.)

Do you think that Zachariah Loussac had more fun making a lot of money or giving a lot of money away? Explain your answer.

_____
_____
_____
_____
_____
_____
_____
_____
_____
_____
_____
_____
_____
_____
_____
_____
_____

ENRICHMENT ACTIVITY

Imagine that you were given $1 million that you could use to help others. How would you spend it? Write a paragraph or two about what you would do with the money.

LEARN MORE

Read more about Z.J. Loussac by visiting http://www.jmaw.org/loussac-jewish-mayor-anchorage-alaska/

UNIT 4: A FEW CITY FOREFATHERS

LESSON 11: "CAP" LATHROP GAMBLES ON ALASKA

FACTS TO KNOW

Austin E. "Cap" Lathrop – One of Alaska's greatest entrepreneurs who became involved in transportation, entertainment, coal and radio, among other things, in Alaska

L.J. Perry – Austin E. "Cap" Lathrop's steamboat

"The Cheechakos" – The first full-length motion picture filmed entirely in Alaska

COMPREHENSION QUESTIONS

1) Why did the discovery of gold in the Turnagain Arm area of Cook Inlet interest Cap Lathrop?

The news interested the Michigan native, not due to the lure of gold, but because the rush offered opportunities in shipping and freighting. (Page 98)

2) Describe the work of a steamboat crew.

A two-boiler boat needed around two cords of wood an hour, around the clock, so the vessels had to stop every 10 to 12 hours for fuel. Boat crews cut wood in the beginning, but soon wood camps were established. The steamboats also had to stop frequently to have their boilers cleaned. This operation took about 10 hours because the fire had to be put out, the boiler cooled and washed, and then river water flushed through to remove mud and debris. (Page 100)

3) Why were movies important in the Last Frontier?

Movies provided a social outlet for people struggling to survive in the Last Frontier. (Page 101)

4) What was the only movie made by the Alaska Motion Picture Corporation? What was it about?

The Cheechakos tells the story of two good-hearted gold prospectors who take in a young girl who was left motherless after a ship explosion. When the sourdoughs strike it rich, the younger miner falls in love with the girl. Through tough experiences, they all learn that disreputable gamblers can be as dangerous as the frozen north. (Pages 103-105)

5) After his movie failed, in what other businesses did Austin Lathrop get involved?
He built a new theater from reinforced concrete, a first in Fairbanks. He also purchased an interest in the Healy River Coal Corporation. Lathrop later built a four-story concrete apartment building, which housed his newly acquired Fairbanks Daily News-Miner newspaper on its first floor. In 1939, he brought radio to the community when he went on the air with KFAR. (Pages 105-108)

DISCUSSION QUESTION

(Discuss this question with your teacher or write your answer in essay form below. Use additional paper if necessary.)

One of the reasons that Austin Lathrop's movie failed in New York was because of the title, *The Cheechakos*. Reread the description of the movie on Pages 106-107. What would you name the movie? Why?

_____
_____
_____
_____
_____
_____
_____
_____
_____
_____
_____
_____
_____
_____
_____
_____
_____
_____

ENRICHMENT ACTIVITY

Watch this short video about the making of Alaska's first full-length motion picture by visiting https://vimeo.com/117362265

LEARN MORE

Read more about steamboat transportation by visiting http://www.akhistorycourse.org/americas-territory/rivers-get-people-and-freight-inland

UNIT 4: A FEW CITY FOREFATHERS

LESSON 12: "MR. BASEBALL" HITS TOWN

FACTS TO KNOW

William F. Mulcahy – Alaska's first National Baseball Congress Commissioner, also known as "Mr. Baseball"

Gertrude Mulcahy – Mr. Baseball's (William Mulcahy) wife

COMPREHENSION QUESTIONS

1) What position led William Mulcahy to move from Connecticut to Anchorage? What common interest did he find with the other railroad workers?
In September 1922, William F. Mulcahy hired on from the New York, New Heaven and Hartford Railway to take the position of station auditor assistant with the Alaska Railroad – he retired as general auditor. He found that he had a common interest in baseball with the other railroad workers. (Pages 110-112)

2) How did he become involved with the baseball league in 1923?
In 1923, Mulcahy became president of the baseball league, as well as its treasurer, secretary, groundskeeper and ticket seller. (Page 112)

3) According to his wife, Gertrude, the railroad company employment manager would ask applicants what position they played in baseball. Why did he ask this question?
Gertrude said, "Most of the work was for unskilled labor, and the employment manager, after reading their applications, would say, 'and what position do you play in baseball?'" The fellows who knew what position they could play were the first ones hired, and they came back each summer during school vacation." (Pages 112-113)

4) What was Gertrude's nickname? Why?
Called "Bill's Bat Boy," Gertrude carried the equipment, balls, tickets and extra wraps to protect the players from the winds that invariably came off the inlet every afternoon. (Page 113)

5) Why did William Mulcahy promote youth sports?
Besides his work with adult baseball, Mulcahy became deeply involved in recreation for the youth of Anchorage. He believed sports to be an answer to the problem of juvenile delinquency and devoted countless hours to promoting sports and facilities for the boys and girls of the city. (Page 114)

6) How did the city of Anchorage honor Mr. Baseball in 1951 and again in 1964?

In 1951, a new baseball stadium was named after him. Considered one of Anchorage's "Grand Old Men," the community wanted to honor the man who, for so many years, stood for baseball in Anchorage. With seating for 750, Mulcahy Stadium held nearly half again as many as the earlier facility. A new stadium at 16th and Gambell, completed in time for the 1964 season, also was given his name. (Page 116)

DISCUSSION QUESTION

(Discuss this question with your teacher or write your answer in essay form below. Use additional paper if necessary.)

Why do you think baseball was such a popular sport for railroad workers?

_____
_____
_____
_____
_____
_____
_____
_____
_____
_____
_____
_____
_____
_____
_____
_____
_____
_____

LEARN MORE

Read about the history of the Alaska Baseball League by visiting http://www.alaskabaseballleague.org/view/alaskabaseballleague/history-127/alaska-baseball-history-2

TIME TO REVIEW

Review Chapters 7-12 of your book before moving on the Unit Review. See how many questions you can answer without looking at your book.

UNIT 3: BIG CITY CONCERNS
UNIT 4: A FEW FOREFATHERS

REVIEW LESSONS 7-12

Write down what you remember about:

Petition – *A formal written request typically signed by many people*

Judge Frederick Brown – *Judge of the Third Judicial Division in Valdez who granted Anchorage residents their first local election*

Mayor Leopold David – *The first mayor of Anchorage*

Prohibition – *A ban on production, transportation and sale of alcoholic beverages*

Anchorage City Council – *Elected city government leaders in Anchorage*

John "Jack" Sturgus – *The first chief of police in Anchorage*

Vice – *Immoral and criminal activities*

Zachariah J. Loussac – *One of Anchorage's first philanthropists*

Philanthropist – *A person who seeks to help others, often by being generous with money*

Austin E. "Cap" Lathrop – *One of Alaska's greatest entrepreneurs who became involved in transportation, entertainment, coal and radio, among other things, in Alaska*

L.J. Perry – *Austin E. "Cap" Lathrop's steamboat*

William F. Mulcahy – *Alaska's first National Baseball Congress Commissioner, also known as "Mr. Baseball"*

Gertrude Mulcahy – *Mr. Baseball's (William Mulcahy) wife*

Fill in the blanks:

1) Technically speaking, Anchorage was born in November _1920_, when a group of Anchorage citizens filed a _petition_ for a special election be held to determine whether the majority of residents wanted the _Alaska Engineering Commission_ to continue to govern the day to day affairs, or if _citizens_ should take over management of the town.

2) The election returns showed a count of _328_ votes for incorporation and _130_ votes against. Another 85 _blank_ ballots had been stuffed into the ballot box. After careful consideration, _Judge Frederick Brown_ ruled the 85 _blank_ votes were to be ignored. Anchorage became a city on Nov. 23, _1920_.

3) When Judge _Leopold David_ became Anchorage's first _elected mayor_, he helped the new city _council_ develop ordinances to provide law and order.

4) Mayor _David_ and the city council tried to curtail _gambling_ by adopting a "c_urtain ordinance_," which required an unobstructed view from the street into "pool halls, cigar stores, soft-drink emporiums, and other businesses of a similar character."

5) Since _bootlegging_ provided a revenue stream for so many of Anchorage's citizens, Mayor _David_, who died of heart disease in 1924 at 43, found it virtually impossible to keep _alcohol_ from flowing in the frontier town.

6) So in an effort to control the _criminal element_ in Anchorage, Mayor _David_ and the _city council_ authorized the establishment of the city's first _police department_ soon after the city became incorporated. But tragedy soon hit that new department. The first _police chief_ was murdered shortly after taking his post.

7) The _Anchorage Daily Times_ offered several _motives_ for the murder of _Jack Sturgus_. One suggested the chief was killed _"while endeavoring to make an arrest or while watching in the rear of the drugstore for some man under suspicion" / "murdered by members of an illicit liquor gang" / "in revenge"_ because of the _"activity of the marshal's office during the past week ...".

8) The _third_ time proved to be the charm for _Zacharia J. Loussac_, when he opened a _drugstore_ in Anchorage. The mushroom growth of Anchorage during _World War II_ was the turning point for his business. Not only was he able to pay off all his debts, but he found money "rolling in by the _bushel baskets_!"

9) In 1946, _Z.J. Loussac_ set up the _Loussac Foundation_, which he dedicated to the recreational, cultural, scientific or educational activities in the _Anchorage_ area. He wanted to do something for _Anchorage_ – the city had been so good to him – and decided to give it _half his wealth_.

10) _Austin "Cap" Lathrop_ plied the waters of Cook Inlet carrying freight and passengers for several years. He also dabbled in _coal, oil and copper_ until the federal government set aside millions of acres of public land for reserves.

11) In 1922, several Anchorage residents decided to go into the _filmmaking_ business themselves. They formed the _Alaska Motion Picture Corporation_ and elected _Austin "Cap" Lathrop_, who owned theaters in Anchorage, Fairbanks, Seward, Valdez and Cordova, as president. The businessmen raised $75,000 (more than $1 million in 2017 dollars) to produce a 12-reel picture titled _The Cheechakos._

12) In September 1922, _William F. Mulcahy_ hired on from the New York, New Heaven and Hartford Railway to take the position of _station auditor assistant_ for the _Alaska Railroad_.

13) In 1923, _William F. Mulcahy_ became president of the _baseball league_, as well as its treasurer, secretary, groundskeeper and ticket seller.

14) Besides his work with adult baseball, _William F. Mulcahy_ became deeply involved in recreation for the _youth_ of Anchorage. He believed sports to be an answer to the problem of _juvenile delinquency_.

Early Alaska Movers & Shakers
Word Scramble Puzzle Key
Unscramble the words below

1.	wraned eicshrnsent	andrew christensen	Land Office chief for Alaska Engineering Commission
2.	crrifdkee nworb	frederick brown	Judge who ordered a special election in Anchorage in 1920
3.	polldoe dviad	leopold david	First elected Anchorage mayor
4.	kafrn erde	frank reed	As a child, he sold bottles to bootleggers
5.	ajkc utssrgu	jack sturgus	First chief of police
6.	csora eorsnadn	oscar anderson	First butcher
7.	hrzcaaia lucsaso	zacharia loussac	Anchorage's first philanthropist
8.	ebn eoebk	ben boeke	City clerk when ZJ Loussac was mayor
9.	**iutans oartlph**	**austin lathrop**	One of Alaska's greatest industrialists
10.	ilwlima ymluhac	william mulcahy	Known as Mr. Baseball

UNIT 3: BIG CITY CONCERNS
UNIT 4: A FEW FOREFATHERS

UNIT TEST

Choose *three* of the following questions to answer in paragraph form. Use as much detail as possible to completely answer the question.

1) Describe how Anchorage residents took over management of their town. What did they do to request an election? What were the results of the election?

2) What were some of the challenges that law enforcement faced in early Anchorage? How did they approach these problems?

3) What happened to the first police chief of Anchorage? Describe some of the theories about this mystery.

4) Summarize the journey of Zachariah Loussac from a poor kid in Russia to a wealthy philanthropist in Alaska. Why is he known as Alaska's first philanthropist?

5) Describe at least two of "Cap" Lanthrop's business ventures. Were these ventures successful? Why or why not?

6) Who was Mr. Baseball? How did he get involved in the baseball league in Alaska? Why did he promote youth sports?

_____

_____

_____

_____

_____

_____

_____

_____

_____

_____

_____

_____

_____

TEACHER NOTES ABOUT THIS UNIT

TEACHER NOTES ABOUT THIS UNIT

Baseball became a popular sport all across Alaska, as seen in this photograph of John Oktollik in the Pribilof Islands in the 1900s.

UNIT 5: TRAILBLAZERS ON WHEELS

LESSON 13: A VERY BUMPY RIDE

FACTS TO KNOW

Robert E. "Bobby" Sheldon – He built the first car in Alaska
Invention – The creation of a device or process after study and experimentation

COMPREHENSION QUESTIONS

1) How much experience did Robert Sheldon have with automobiles before building the first car in Alaska? How did he learn how to build a car?
Sheldon, who'd never seen an automobile, described his creation: "All I knew about them was what I read in papers from the states. I was interested in mechanics, and being on the night shift at the Skagway powerhouse, I had considerable time to think it over." In his spare time, the natural mechanic read everything he could lay his hands on and quietly started taking correspondence courses. (Pages 118-119)

2) What was Robert Sheldon's first job at age 14? What first did he accomplish in this job?
Sheldon got a job selling newspapers and had the distinction of being the first newsboy in Alaska to sell a paper to the notorious criminal Soapy Smith. Sheldon later said: "Soapy always gave me $1 for his paper. The regular price was two bits. As you can imagine, I was very sorry when Soapy was shot by the vigilantes!" (Page 119)

3) What inspired Robert Sheldon to build a car?
"There was this beautiful girl there in Skagway, and I was trying to beat another fellow's time," Sheldon said. "He was the son of a banker and had the use of his father's horse and buggy, which was a luxury in those days. I didn't have a horse and buggy and had no immediate prospects of getting either. One night I had the idea of building one of those new gasoline engine-powered buggies I had been reading about. ..." (Page 120)

4) Why did he quit his job at Northern Commercial Power Plant? What "impossible" task did he set out to do in 1913?
The lucrative possibilities of commercial transportation weren't lost on the entrepreneur. Sheldon quit his job with Northern Commercial, and along with three passengers, he set out on July 29, 1913, to try the impossible – travel by car over the primitive wagon trail from Fairbanks to Valdez. (Pages 121-122)

5) What business did Sheldon start after becoming the first man to ride a bike from Valdez to Fairbanks?

When he returned to Fairbanks, Sheldon ordered more Model-Ts and organized Sheldon's Auto-Stage Line, which he operated with various partners until 1926. The company averaged three trips a month and those excursions were rugged any time of year. (Page 122)

6) When he left the transportation business in 1926, what did he do for work?

Sheldon left the transportation business in 1926 to chalk up another first – a tourist concession in McKinley Park (now Denali National Park and Preserve), which he operated until 1931. (Pages 124-125)

DISCUSSION QUESTION

(Discuss this question with your teacher or write your answer in essay form below. Use additional paper if necessary.)

Robert Sheldon often said, "Who wants to be the richest man in the cemetery?" What do you think he meant by this question?

_____
_____
_____
_____
_____
_____
_____
_____
_____
_____
_____
_____
_____
_____

ENRICHMENT ACTIVITY

Read more about Model-T cars and how they changed America by visiting http://www.history.com/topics/automobiles

LEARN MORE

Look for this article at your local library:
"But We Kept 'em Going," in THE ALASKA JOURNAL 11 (1981): 237-240.
Monaghan, Patricia and Roland Wulbert

UNIT 5: TRAILBLAZERS ON WHEELS

LESSON 14: A REO AND A RESORT
LESSON 15: ALASKA'S FIRST STREETCAR

Note: Read both chapters 14 and 15 before completing this lesson.

FACTS TO KNOW

Joe Spenard – He drove the first auto truck in Anchorage and ran a taxi service
Lake Spenard – Anchorage lakeside resort that Joe Spenard opened in 1916
Martin Itjen – Built, owned and operated a streetcar in Skagway

COMPREHENSION QUESTIONS

1) What did Joe Spenard do after moving from Valdez to Anchorage?
Once he got settled in the new town, he purchased his truck – said to be the first auto truck in Anchorage. Spenard started a taxi service with a Model-T Ford, too, and plastered lost and found notices and tide information on the sides of that vehicle. (Pages 128-129)

2) Why was the area known as "Miracle Mile" important to the growth of Anchorage?
As part of the Chugach National Forest created by U.S. President Theodore "Teddy" Roosevelt in 1907, the land was locked in a government deep freeze. In 1919, this piece of land was liberated after the Alaska Railroad camp of Anchorage was born, and its residents asked that the surrounding land be unshackled. The growth of Anchorage to the south would not have occurred if this "miracle" hadn't happened. (Pages 129-131)

3) What discovery did Joe Spenard make as he was clearing trees? What did he do after he made this discovery?
Spenard found a beautiful lake a few miles from the railroad community. There he set up a camp. He also made improvements to the land, which included a fullscale resort with a roadhouse, bathhouses and a swimming beach. He opened his recreational resort in August 1916. (Pages 131-132)

4) Why did he sell the resort in 1917? What happened to Lake Spenard after Joe left?
Spenard's health was poor and he had to leave Alaska in September 1917. He sold his Reo and headed for California to seek medical treatment for a heart condition. After he left, his resort thrived and the trail Spenard cut through the wilderness became one of the busiest roads in Alaska. The strange, beautiful lake he claimed is now called Lake Spenard and is surrounded by business, recreation and transportation. (Page 132)

5) What led Martin Itjen to start Skagway Streetcar Company?
Martin took U.S. President Warren G. Harding on an excursion in a painted coal truck. After seeing how much Harding enjoyed the tour, Itjen figured he could make a living off tourism in the gold rush city and started the Skagway Streetcar Company. (Page 134)

6) How did Martin Itjen entertain his customers? What were his streetcars like?
One picturesque car carried a bear cub replica on the front that growled and pointed to the left or right as the car turned. He also had a lifesize mannequin of Soapy Smith that performed when Itjen worked a series of foot pedals. It nodded its head, waved a flag, rang a bell and puffed exhaust smoke through a cigarette. Itjen gave his customers quite a show as he recited poetry, told stories. (Page 136)

7) Why did Martin Itjen travel to Hollywood, California?
Itjen traveled to Hollywood to extend an invitation to movie star Mae West to come north. Itjen drove his streetcar to California and spent two weeks with West, but he couldn't convince her to come north with him to be a hostess on his streetcar. (Pages 136-137)

DISCUSSION QUESTION

(Discuss this question with your teacher or write your answer in essay form below. Use additional paper if necessary.)

What type of transportation did Alaskans rely on before motorized vehicles? Name some of the ways that motorized vehicles changed their way of life.

_____
_____
_____
_____
_____

ENRICHMENT ACTIVITY

Have you ever wondered who invented an everyday item like your bicycle, eyeglasses, pencil or refrigerator? Spend some time at your local library to research three common, everyday items and the people that invented them. Take notes on what you learn. Present what you learn to the class.

LEARN MORE

Read more about early automobiles in Alaska by visiting
http://www.akhistorycourse.org/americas-territory/overland-routes-develop

Early Transportation in Alaska
Word Search Puzzle Key
Find the words listed below

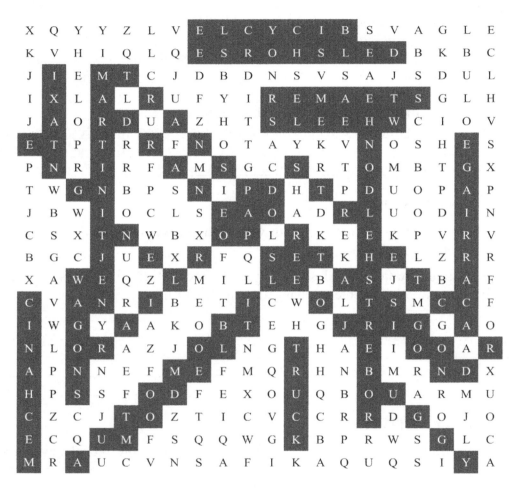

ROBERT SHELDON	JOE SPENARD	MARTIN ITJEN
BUGGY	WHEELS	ENGINE
WAGONS	SLED	DOGS
MECHANIC	STEAMER	RAILROAD
TRANSPORTATION	AUTOMOBILE	MODEL T
HORSE	BICYCLE	TRUCK
TAXI	STREETCAR	CARRIAGE

While automobiles brought a new way to travel around Alaska, as seen in the photograph above of a loaded Model T touring car in front of a roadhouse, the lack of proper roads caused some problems, as seen in the photo below of a Model T stuck in mud.

UNIT 6: EPIDEMICS, RESCUES AND DISASTER

LESSON 16: THE BIG SICKNESS

FACTS TO KNOW

Influenza – Contagious viral infection that often occurs in epidemics
Epidemic – Widespread occurrence of a disease in a community at the same time
Thomas Riggs – Governor of Alaska Territory from 1918 to 1921

COMPREHENSION QUESTIONS

1) Called the *Spanish flu*, only because the *Spanish* press wrote about it, the virus took more than *500,000* American lives between 1918-1919. Fatality estimates worldwide range from *20* million to *100* million.

2) How did Alaska Territorial Gov. Thomas Riggs attempt to keep influenza away from Alaska's residents?
Riggs asked steamship companies to examine all passengers heading north on the final ships of the season. He warned that anyone showing signs of influenza would be isolated at the port of debarkation and assigned physicians to meet the ships and enforce his directive. He advised Native people to stay in their own villages and repel all visitors; to avoid visiting one another's homes within their villages; indeed, to avoid all gatherings, even those most vital to their self-esteem. (Pages 139-143)

3) What caused influenza to rapidly spread in the Seward Peninsula?
When passengers from the S.S. Victoria, the last ship of the season from Seattle, docked in Nome, the killer disease enveloped the Seward Peninsula. And when the Victoria arrived in Nome on Oct. 20, all those who came ashore were quarantined in the hospital for five days and all freight and mail were fumigated. Within days, Alaska Natives were sick and dying. In a single eight-day period, 162 had died. (Pages 140-141)

4) What previous events caused the Native people of Alaska to fear sickness brought by non-Natives? Describe some of the Alaska Natives' beliefs about sickness.
Earlier epidemics of smallpox, measles and typhoid fever had instilled a paralyzing fear in Alaska's Native population. They believed in the spirit of death and feared that, if a person died in their home, that spirit would claim them next. (Page 141)

5) How did Gov. Thomas Riggs describe the flu epidemic in Alaska?
"I doubt if similar conditions existed anywhere in the world – the intense cold of the arctic days, the long distances to be traveled by dog team, the living children huddled against

66

their dead parents already being gnawed by wolfish dogs," he said in his annual report to the Secretary of the Interior. Riggs suggested that those in power who should have helped Alaskans were "all too much engrossed with the woes of Europe to be able to note our wards, seemingly protected by solemn treaty with Russia, dying by swarms in the dark of the northern nights." (Page 148)

DISCUSSION QUESTION

(Discuss this question with your teacher or write your answer in essay form below. Use additional paper if necessary.)

Why do you think influenza does not kill as many people today as it did between 1918-1919?

_____
_____
_____
_____
_____
_____
_____
_____
_____
_____
_____
_____
_____
_____
_____
_____

ENRICHMENT ACTIVITY

Imagine that you are a doctor in 1918 during the influenza epidemic. Create a poster to educate the public about ways that they can prevent the flu. Consider what you know about how to protect yourself from catching the flu. Keep in mind that the first flu vaccines were not developed until the 1930s.

LEARN MORE

Read more about the influenza epidemic and other diseases that affected early Alaska history by visiting http://www.akhistorycourse.org/americas-territory/alaskas-heritage/chapter-4-21-health-and-medicine

UNIT 6: EPIDEMICS, RESCUES AND DISASTER

LESSON 17: DISASTER STRIKES SOUTHEAST

FACTS TO KNOW

Princess Sophia – Canadian steamer that sunk in 1918 killing more than 350 people
Captain Leonard Locke – Captain of the *Princess Sophia*
Vanderbilt Reef – Rocky area just visible above the water's surface in Southeast Alaska's Lynn Canal

COMPREHENSION QUESTIONS

1) Who was traveling on the *Princess Sophia* when it pulled out of the port at Skagway in October 1918?
The ship was filled with 350 gold miners, families and others heading south for the winter. The steamship company, in an effort to hold more passengers for the voyage, had converted the Sophia so she could carry 100 more passengers than normal. (Page 150)

2) Describe the *Princess Sophia*. Was it considered a safe ship?
It was considered a sturdy ship. "She was not a beautiful princess but a sturdy, somewhat chunky down to earth lady of the seas," wrote Ian MacDonald and Betty O'Keefe in their book, The Final Voyage of the Princess Sophia. "She was practical, comfortable and soon became popular with those who traveled the West Coast to Alaska," (Page 150)

3) What was the weather like a few hours after the steamer left Skagway? How did the ship get off course?
About four hours out of Skagway, Capt. Leonard Locke ran into a north wind that began pushing the Sophia southward. "The weather suddenly worsened and a blinding snow-storm overtook the ship from the north," wrote Ken Coates and Bill Morrison in their book, The Sinking of the Princess Sophia: Taking the North Down With Her. (Page 152)

4) What happened when the *Princess Sophia* reached Vanderbilt Reef at 2 a.m?
By 2 a.m. on Oct. 24, the Sophia was steaming into an area known as Vanderbilt Reef. And unbeknownst to Locke, a navigation error had placed the ship two miles off course. Sophia struck the reef at 2:10 a.m. "Because the reef was so low in the water the bow lifted out of the water and, with a horrible grinding and tearing, slid up and onto the rock." (Page 153)

5) How did the *Princess Sophia* sink? Did anyone survive?

About 40 hours after she settled on the rocks, the sea picked up Sophia's stern and turned her 180 degrees, slipping her off the reef – tearing her bottom out as she went – and eventually covered her in the frigid froth. Those on support vessels returning the next day were horrified to see only her mast standing out of the water. There was only one survivor, a dog that swam ashore. (Pages 154-155)

DISCUSSION QUESTION

(Discuss this question with your teacher or write your answer in essay form below. Use additional paper if necessary.)

Why was the sinking of the *Princess Sophia* devastating to Dawson City?

_____
_____
_____
_____
_____
_____
_____
_____
_____
_____
_____
_____
_____
_____
_____
_____
_____

ENRICHMENT ACTIVITY

Watch this short YouTube video to learn more about the *Princess Sophia* tragedy:
https://www.youtube.com/watch?v=S3DSMyZb5dc

LEARN MORE

Look for this book at your local library:
SOS North Pacific, Gordon R. Newell. Portland, Oregon: Binford and Mort, 1955.

UNIT 6: EPIDEMICS, RESCUES AND DISASTER

LESSON 18: FIRST RELAY RUN NORTH

FACTS TO KNOW

Dr. John B. Beeson – Alaska railroad doctor who traveled 500 miles on the Iditarod Trail to help Claude Baker
Claude Baker – Iditarod banker who was near death from an injury in 1921

COMPREHENSION QUESTIONS

1) Why did Dr. John Beeson travel to Iditarod in 1921?
Dr. Beeson traveled to help Claude Baker who was suffering from an old injury he'd received while serving as a guard on the gold trail outside of the famous mining town. The banker also had a lung ailment. (Pages 158-159)

2) How did he travel there?
Beeson's trip began with a train ride, a dog team and another train ride between Anchorage and Nenana. Then a relay of dog teams and sleds took him the rest of the way to Iditarod. (Pages 158-159)

3) How long did it take him to get to Iditarod? Who helped the dog team relay to run smoothly?
The trip took five and a half days after the train ride to Nenana. Thanks to headquarters' managers of the Northern Commercial Company, Messrs. Goss at Tanana, Parsons at Ruby and Sam Applebaum at Iditarod, teams had been ready and equipped at points along the way to aid Beeson on his journey to Iditarod. (Pages 163-164)

4) How was the return trip different?
It took Beeson 14 days to reach the railroad on his trip out with his patient due to extreme freezing temperatures. (Pages 164-165)

DISCUSSION QUESTION

(Discuss this question with your teacher or write your answer in essay form below. Use additional paper if necessary.)

What do you think the definition of a hero is? Would you call Dr. Beeson a hero? Why or why not?

70

LEARN MORE

Learn more about ways that Alaska Natives promoted health, reduced pain and met the challenges of life by visiting http://www.akhistorycourse.org/alaskas-cultures/alaska-natives-and-health

MAP ACTIVITY

Using the map below, trace Dr. Beeson's route after he got off the railroad train in Nenana. Find the following places he raced through on his way to save the banker's life in Iditarod: 1) Manley Hot Springs   2) Tanana   3) Ruby   4) Poorman   5) Cripple 6) Ophir   7) Iditarod

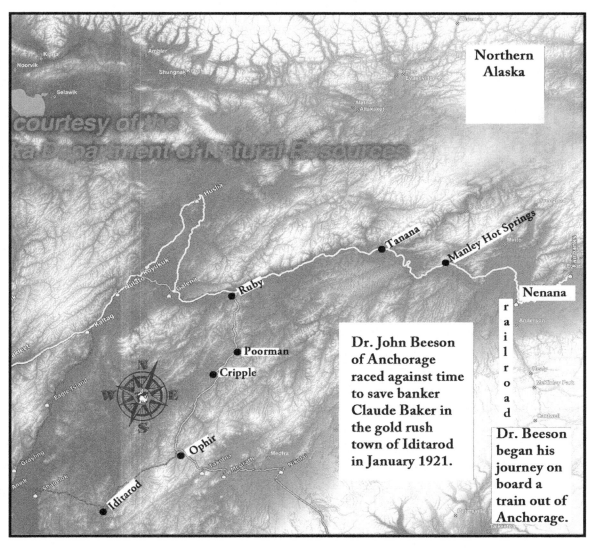

Northern Alaska

Dr. John Beeson of Anchorage raced against time to save banker Claude Baker in the gold rush town of Iditarod in January 1921.

Dr. Beeson began his journey on board a train out of Anchorage.

UNIT 6: EPIDEMICS, RESCUES AND DISASTER

LESSON 19: DIPHTHERIA THREATENS NOME

FACTS TO KNOW

Diphtheria – Highly contagious disease that killed several people in Nome in the 1920s

Dr. Curtis Welch – Physician in Nome who sent for antitoxin to stop the diphtheria outbreak there

Leonhard Seppala – Legendary musher who helped carry the diphtheria serum to Nome

COMPREHENSION QUESTIONS

1) What did Dr. Curtis Welch do when he saw the grayish patches of diphtheria membranes in 7-year-old Bessie Stanley on Jan. 2, 1925?
He only had enough antitoxin, which is made from the serum of immunized horses, for a few people. So along with instituting quarantines, Welch sent radio telegrams via the U.S. Army Signal Corps to all the major towns and officials in Alaska. He desperately needed serum. (Page 166)

2) How is diphtheria spread from person to person? What is the cure?
Diphtheria is highly contagious, easily passing from one person to another through coughs, sneezes, or even through laughing. Antitoxin is the cure. (Page 166)

3) Why did Dr. Welch expect that there would be a large number of deaths in Alaska's Native population of Nome without the antitoxin?
The doctor knew that Alaska's first people lacked resistance to white man's diseases. A previous influenza epidemic in 1918-1919 wiped out about 50 percent of the Native residents in Nome, and 8 percent of the Native population throughout Alaska. Without antitoxin, expected deaths from this diphtheria outbreak was high. (Page 167)

4) Who was able to send the first shipment of antitoxin to Nome in 1921? How long did it take to get there?
Luckily, on Jan. 26 Anchorage physician John B. Beeson found 300,000 units of serum in the Alaska Railroad Hospital. Together, mushers and their dog teams covered the route in 127-1/2 hours, which was considered a world record, all driven in subzero temperatures in near-blizzard conditions and hurricane-force winds. (Pages 168-181)

72

5) Who were Balto and Togo? Why were they considered the real heroes of the relay teams that brought the antitoxin to Nome? How were they honored after the serum was delivered to Nome?

Balto and Togo were two of the many sled dogs who raced to bring diphtheria serum to Nome through storms and freezing conditions. Some of the dogs lost their lives during the trip. After the town of Nome was saved, the sled dogs were taken on promotional tours where thousands of people came to see them. There was a statue built to honor Balto in New York City's Central Park. Togo, Leonhard Seppala's lead dog, was stuffed and is on display at the Iditarod Museum in Wasilla. (Pages 174-181)

DISCUSSION QUESTION

(Discuss this question with your teacher or write your answer in essay form below. Use additional paper if necessary.)

What did you learn about dogs in this lesson? Why do you think they were the best kind of animal to pull sleds as means of long-distance transportation in Alaska?

_____
_____
_____
_____
_____
_____
_____
_____
_____
_____
_____
_____
_____
_____
_____
_____

LEARN MORE

Look for this book at your local library:
Everything I Know About Training and Racing Sled Dogs, George Attla. Rome, New York: Arner Publications, 1974

TIME TO REVIEW

Review Chapters 13-19 of your book before moving on the Unit Review. See how many questions you can answer without looking at your book.

Epidemics, Rescues and Disasters
Crossword Puzzle

Read Across and Down clues and fill in blank boxes that match numbers on the clues

Across

3   Infectious disease that spreads widely and affects many people at the same time
5   Alaska village where scientists unearthed victims of the 1918 flu in the late 1990s to study their DNA
8   Musher that took serum from Nenana to Minto and was first musher in the relay toward Nome
10 Captain of the steamship that hit reef in Southeast Alaska in 1918
12 Alaska governor who tried to keep flu away from the north
15 Alaska governor when 1925 serum run to Nome happened
18 Nurse who helped doctor in Nome diagnose sick people in 1925
20 Method by which doctor traveled to Iditarod to save banker's life
22 Name of reef that the steamship hit in October 1918
24 First man to summit Denali who was on board the ship that sank in Southeast Alaska in 1918
25 A strict isolation imposed to prevent the spread of disease
27 Famous serum-run dog is stuffed and on display at the Iditarod Museum in this Alaska town
28 Banker who was desperately ill in Iditarod in January 1921
29 Doctor's first time mushing was because this fellow misjudged a turn and crashed on the way to Iditarod to save a banker's life
32 Doctor who raced from Anchorage to Iditarod to save a banker's life
34 Condition when wind and blowing snow made it difficult for dogs and mushers to see the trail on the way to Nome in 1925
35 A group of people or animals engaged in a task or activity for a fixed period of time and then replaced by a similar group
37 Lead dog that pulled into Nome with life-saving serum on Feb. 2, 1925
38 Place where Leonhard Seppala is buried
39 First reported case of flu in Alaska was in this town

Down

1   Sole survivor of the ship that sunk in Southeast Alaska in October 1918
2   These people were suspected of carrying the flu to several Alaska villages
4   Steamship that sank in Southeast Alaska in October 1918
6   Ship that carried flu to Nome in October 1918
7   Flu never made it to this northern Alaska village because of strict quarantine
9   Famous musher who helped doctor get back to Anchorage after saving the banker in Iditarod
11 Flu that killed millions during 1918-1919
13 About $1 million of this ore was on board the steamship that sank in Southeast Alaska in 1918
14 Type of sled dog
16 People feared that this would spread like wildlife in Nome in 1925

Epidemics, Rescues and Disasters
Crossword Puzzle Key

Down (Continued)

17 Leonhard Seppala's lead dog that traveled two to three times farther than any other dog team in the serum relay to Nome

19 Musher who pulled onto Front Street in Nome with the serum to save lives in February 1925

21 Alaska Railroad conductor who carried the serum from Anchorage to Nenana in 1925

23 Village where Dr. Curtis Welch saw symptoms of tonsillitis in 2-year old Inuit girl who then died in January 1925

26 Alaska village that paired men and women for marriage so orphans of the flu epidemic would have homes

30 River on which the doctor traveled to get to Iditarod in 1921

31 This is made from the serum of immunized horses and helps stop disease

33 Medicine that is injected into someone's blood to protect them against a poison or disease

36 Everyone in this Alaska village died from the flu of 1918

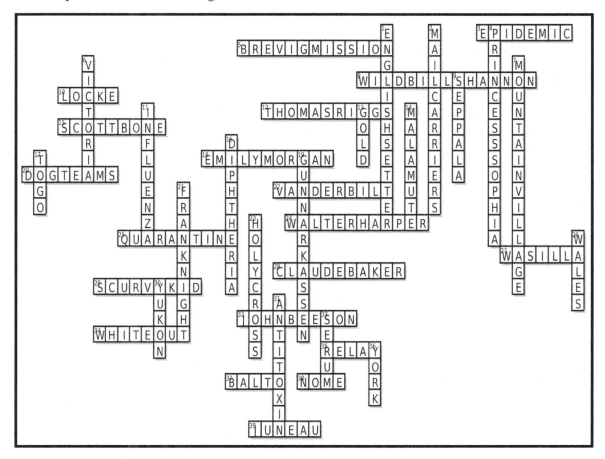

UNIT 5: TRAILBLAZERS ON WHEELS
UNIT 6: EPIDEMICS, RESCUES AND DISASTER

REVIEW LESSONS 13-19

Write down what you remember about:

Robert E. "Bobby" Sheldon – *He built the first car in Alaska*

Invention – *The creation of a device or process after study and experimentation*

Joe Spenard – *Drove the first auto truck in Anchorage and ran a taxi service*

Lake Spenard – *Anchorage lakeside resort that Joe Spenard opened in 1916*

Martin Itjen – *Built, owned and operated a streetcar in Skagway*

Influenza – *Contagious viral infection that often occurs in epidemics*

Epidemic – *Widespread occurrence of a disease in a community at the same time*

Thomas Riggs – *Governor of Alaska Territory from 1918 to 1921*

Princess Sophia – *Canadian steamer that sunk in 1918 killing more than 350 people*

Captain Leonard Locke – *Captain of the Princess Sophia*

Vanderbilt Reef – *Rocky area just visible above the water's surface in the Lynn Canal*

Dr. John B. Beeson – *Alaska railroad doctor who traveled 500 miles on the Iditarod Trail to help Claude Baker*

Claude Baker – *Iditarod banker who was near death from an injury*

Diphtheria – *Highly contagious disease that killed several people in Nome in the 1920s*

Dr. Curtis Welch – *Physician in Nome who sent for antitoxin to stop the diphtheria outbreak there*

Leonhard Seppala – *Legendary musher who helped carry the diphtheria serum to Nome*

Fill in the blanks:

1) On July 29, 1913, one of Alaska's trailblazers started on a historic journey – the first _automobile_ trip over the wagon trail from _Fairbanks_ to _Valdez_. But that wasn't _Robert E. "Bobby" Sheldon's_ first experience with a _motorized vehicle_. _Sheldon_, who'd never seen an _automobile_, also built the first _car_ in Alaska.

2) Shortly after arriving in _Valdez_, _Sheldon_ sold the Model-T for $1,300 and bought a _bicycle_. He then pedaled back to _Fairbanks_ to become the first person to ride a _bike_ from _Valdez_ to the interior city. When he returned to _Fairbanks_, _Sheldon_ ordered more Model-Ts and organized _Sheldon's Auto-Stage Line_.

3) _Joe Spenard_ moved to Anchorage from Valdez, where he'd had a small transfer business. Once he got settled in the new town, he purchased his _truck_ – said to be the first _auto truck_ in Anchorage.

4) While wandering through the timbered land one day, _Joe Spenard_ found a _beautiful lake_ a few miles from the railroad community. There he set up a camp. He also made improvements to the land, which included a _full-scale resort_ with a roadhouse, bath-houses and a swimming beach. The area become known as _Lake Spenard_.

5) _Martin Itjen_, an immigrant who came north from Florida in 1898 to join the stampede in search of riches in the _Klondike_, took _President Warren G. Harding_ on an excursion in a painted coal truck. After seeing how much _Harding_ enjoyed the tour, he figured he could make a living off tourism in the famous gold rush city and started the _Skagway Streetcar Company._

6) In Alaska's only _streetcar_, 65-year-old sourdough _Martin Itjen_, who was _Skagway_'s undertaker in the roaring days of the gold rush, traveled to the Continental United States to see _Mae West_, the movie actress.

7) During the spring of 1918, a _flu_ had spread across the world and sickened many people – and many died. Called the _Spanish flu_, only because the Spanish press wrote about it, the virus took more than 500,000 American lives between _1918-1919_. Deaths worldwide range from _20_ million to _100_ million.

8) Alaska Gov. _Thomas Riggs_, who recognized that the deeply rooted Native culture of _hospitality and gathering together_ might be aiding in the spread of the disease, issued a directive on Nov. 7 to try and stem the tide of Native deaths. He advised them "to _stay in their own villages_ and repel all _visitors_; to avoid _visiting one another's homes_ within their villages; indeed, to avoid all _gatherings_, even those most vital to their self-esteem.

9) The Canadian Pacific Railway steamship _Princess Sophia_ pulled out of the port at _Skagway_ around 10 p.m. on Oct. 23, 1918, and headed into the _Lynn_ Canal bound for Vancouver. One of the last ships scheduled to leave that fall, the 245-foot ship was filled with _350_ gold miners, families and others heading south for the winter.

10) About 40 hours after she settled on the _rocks_, the sea picked up _Sophia_'s stern and turned her 180 degrees, slipping her off the _reef_ – tearing her bottom out as she went. The sinking of the _Princess Sophia_ devastated _Dawson_ City, as many of its professionals and businesspeople were on board the ill-fated steamer. It also was reported that _$1 million in gold_ was in her hold.

11) Early on the morning of Jan. 24, 1921, _Dr. John B. Beeson_ hopped on a train leaving _Anchorage_ and headed toward _Iditarod_ after getting word through the U.S. Army Signal Corps that _banker Claude Baker_ was near death.

12) _Dr. John Beeson_ pulled into _Iditarod_, by _dog team_, five and a half days after stepping off the train in _Nenana_.

13) When _Dr. Curtis Welch_ saw the grayish patches of _diphtheria_ membranes in 7-year-old Bessie Stanley on Jan. 21, 1925, he sounded the alarm that triggered a race against time to stop a massive outbreak. Along with instituting _quarantines_, _Welch_ sent radio telegrams via the U.S. Army Signal Corps to all the major towns and officials in Alaska. He desperately needed _antitoxin/serum_.

14) The dog teams that carried the life-saving _serum_ would follow the _mail route_ from _Nenana to Nome_, which crossed the barren Alaska Interior, following the _Tanana_ River for 137 miles to the village of _Tanana_ at the junction with the Yukon River.

Gunnar Kasson & Balto
in their Race to Nome.

UNIT 5: TRAILBLAZERS ON WHEELS
UNIT 6: EPIDEMICS, RESCUES AND DISASTER

Unit Test

Choose *three* of the following questions to answer in paragraph form. Use as much detail as possible to completely answer the question.

1) What famous firsts did Robert Sheldon accomplish? Describe how he learned how to do these things.

2) What discovery did Joe Spenard make? How did he make this discovery? What did he do after he made this discovery?

3) What business did Martin Itjen start in Skagway? How did he come up with the idea? Why did he travel to Hollywood?

4) What epidemic took millions of lives around the world between 1918-1919? How did this epidemic affect Alaska? What did the governor do to try to stop the spread of this disease? How did it eventually stop?

5) Explain what happened to the *Princess Sophia* in October 1918. Why was this event devastating to Dawson City?

6) Why did Alaska Natives fear disease brought by Europeans? What did they believe about disease? What precautions were taken to stop the spread of disease among Native people?

7) Why were sled dogs considered heroes to many people in 1925? How were they honored around the United States?

_____
_____
_____
_____
_____
_____
_____
_____
_____

TEACHER NOTES ABOUT THIS UNIT

TEACHER NOTES ABOUT THIS UNIT

Courtesy Wikipedia

Lake Hood Seaplane Base started out as two smaller lakes: Lake Hood to the west and Lake Spenard, discovered by Joe Spenard in the early 1900s, to the east. The state began dredging out a canal in between the two to create seaplane takeoff and taxi lanes in the 1970s. Today, Lake Hood sees nearly 200 daily operations and has become the largest and busiest seaplane base in the world.

UNIT 7: EARLY ALASKA AVIATION

LESSON 20: MAGNIFICENT FLYING MACHINES

FACTS TO KNOW

Henry Peterson – Built Alaska's first airplane
Arthur Williams – Organized the first air show in Alaska with James Martin
James V. Martin – The first to fly in Alaska's skies
Black Wolf Squadron – Alaska flying expedition organized by Brig. Gen. William Mitchell

COMPREHENSION QUESTIONS

1) Who was the first man to venture into Alaska's skies on July 4, 1899?
"Professor" Leonard ascended to 1,000 feet over Juneau in a hot-air balloon he designed, according to Robert W. Stevens, author of Alaskan Aviation History. (Page 187)

2) How did Henry Peterson build Alaska's first airplane? What was the plane like? What was the first flight like? *Peterson ordered a set of plans and a motor from Outside. He then built his machine inside the old Ames Mercantile Company warehouse. The plane, equipped with sled runners for mobility, was towed to an open area. The would-be pilot, who had no flying experience but had read much about constructing and operating the plane, attempted lift off. But the machine did not budge. (Page 188)*

3) Where did the first flight over Alaska take place? How did Arthur Williams get involved in it? *The first actual flight in Alaska soared in Fairbanks in 1913, when Arthur Williams, owner of the Arcade Café, and R.S. McDonald brought aviator James V. Martin north. The promoters thought they'd make a hefty profit with a Fourth of July air show. (Page 189)*

4) Why did Brig. Gen William Mitchell organize the Black Wolf Squadron?
The general wanted to show that airplanes could play an integral part in the nation's defense. The Alaska flying expedition was named the Black Wolf Squadron. The group set out from New York on July 15, 1920, to "demonstrate that we could establish an airway to Alaska and Asia," according to Alaskan Aviation History author Stevens. (Page 189)

DISCUSSION QUESTION

(Discuss this question with your teacher or write your answer in essay form below. Use additional paper if necessary.)

What do you think are some of the benefits of air travel over other methods of transportation?

_____

_____

_____

_____

_____

_____

_____

_____

_____

_____

_____

_____

_____

_____

_____

_____

_____

_____

ENRICHMENT ACTIVITY

Alaska's first flight was big news in 1920. Imagine that you are the journalist who got an exclusive interview with pilot James Martin. Write down 3-5 questions that you would ask him. Can you imagine how he might answer the questions?

LEARN MORE

Read more about early air transportation in Alaska by visiting http://www.akhistory-course.org/americas-territory/alaskas-heritage/chapter-4-12-air-transportation

UNIT 7: EARLY ALASKA AVIATION

LESSON 21: AVIATORS HEAD NORTH

FACTS TO KNOW

Aviator – A pilot, airman or airwoman
Charles Otis Hammontree – The first aviator to fly an amphibian aircraft in Anchorage
Roy Franklin Jones – Cook Inlet aviator who started a flying service in Ketchikan
Merle Sasseen – Well-known bush pilot

COMPREHENSION QUESTIONS

1) Describe Anchorage's first flight. Who flew the plane? What kind of plane was it? How did the aviator prepare for the flight? *Charles Otis Hammontree flew the first plane in Anchorage. He called the Boeing C-11S biplane, with a 100-horsepower motor, "Mudhen" in honor of the mudflats surrounding Anchorage. He had the plane sent from Bremerton, Washington, and assembled it on the Old Dock. On Monday, May 22, 1922, an Alaska Engineering Commission crane lowered the 2,400-pound seaplane into the water. Hammontree ran the new motor for several hours to break it in and he flew the plane for the first time on Friday, June 24. (Pages 196-197)*

2) Why did Roy Jones see a need for a flying service in Ketchikan? Why did he close the business after only a year and a half? *The young aviator moved to Ketchikan, and after seeing a need for aerial surveys for the fishery, timber and other resources, he decided the area could use a flying service. After a year and a half, it appears that the problems of operating those early planes, along with the liquid-cooled motors, were too difficult in Southeast Alaska. (Pages 197-198)*

3) How was the first landing strip in Anchorage made? Who was the first aviator to use it? *Arthur Shonbeck organized and led the entire town in clearing a field of trees, stumps and moss just beyond civilization. The cleared strip along Ninth and 10th avenues not only became an airstrip for bush pilots, it also turned into a nine-hole golf course. Noel Wien was the first to use the landing field. (Page 200)*

4) What "mishaps" did Merle Sasseen have? *Merle Sasseen survived three crashes in as many months, two of which while landing on the "runway" at Anchorage's out-of-town field. (Page 203)*

5) How did Alaskan pilots typically dress to fly the early open-cockpit planes? *A typical aviator outfit included two pairs of heavy wool socks, one pair of caribou-skin socks, moccasins that reached over the knees, heavy underwear, a pair of breeches, a pair of heavy trousers, a shirt and sweater, a skin cap and goggles. The whole outfit then was covered with a knee-length fur or skin parka. Wool gloves covered with heavy fur mitts protected their hands.* (Page 202)

DISCUSSION QUESTION

(Discuss this question with your teacher or write your answer in essay form below. Use additional paper if necessary.)

Why do think that towns like Fairbanks and Ketchikan held large celebrations when the first aircraft landed in their city?

_____
_____
_____
_____
_____
_____
_____
_____
_____
_____
_____
_____
_____

ENRICHMENT ACTIVITY

History is made up of numerous cause-and-effect relationships. No historical event happens in isolation. Part of historical study is learning how people, places, movements and events are interrelated. Consider what you have learned thus far about the history of Alaska. Write five cause-and-effect relationships that you notice from your reading. Example: After the Wright Brothers made the first flight in 1903, flying events began popping up across the country.

LEARN MORE

TOP COVER FOR AMERICA: THE AIR FORCE IN ALASKA, by John Haile Cloe and Michael F. Monaghan 1920-1983. Missoula, Montana: Pictorial Histories Publishing Company, 1984.

UNIT 7: EARLY ALASKA AVIATION

LESSON 22: STRANGE SIGHT SOARS OVER TELLER

FACTS TO KNOW

Dirigible – A lighter-than-air craft that is powered and steerable
Norge – Dirigible from Norway that traveled to the North Pole in 1926
Roald Amundsen – Famous explorer who traveled from Norway to Alaska in the
Norge

COMPREHENSION QUESTIONS

1) The *dirigible* *Norge* left *Norway* to travel across the *North Pole* on May 11, 1926.

2) How did the city of Nome prepare for the arrival of *Norge*? *They decorated their fine city, set up committees, arranged receptions and lined up wagon teams to take schoolchildren to the airfield to see the landing of the dirigible Norge N-1. (Page 202)*

3) What happened when the aircraft got to Alaska? How did it end up off course? *After several hours, it ran into fog and suffered icing problems. Then harsh winds blew it off course. (Page 205)*

4) What did the crewmembers do with the *Norge* when it reached Teller? *The crew of the Norge salvaged the main components of the dirigible after landing in Teller. Those parts then were shipped back to Europe. The silver fabric that covered the craft was cut into pieces, and many Alaskans ended up with a piece of material as a souvenir of the event. (Page 208)*

5) What did this expedition over the North Pole confirm? *Amundsen and his team's expedition over the North Pole confirmed that no land lay between the pole and Alaska in the Arctic Ocean. (Page 208)*

DISCUSSION QUESTION

(Discuss this question with your teacher or write your answer in essay form below. Use additional paper if necessary.)

The introduction of air travel was big news in Alaska and all over the world. What new invention or technology is making big news today?

_____
_____
_____
_____
_____
_____
_____
_____
_____
_____
_____
_____
_____
_____
_____
_____

LEARN MORE

Read more about the history of flight by visiting https://www.grc.nasa.gov/WWW/K-12/UEET/StudentSite/historyofflight.html

MAP ACTIVITY

Locate the following places that you have been reading about in this unit on the map below: 1) Fairbanks   2) Anchorage   3) Ketchikan   4) Nome   5) Teller

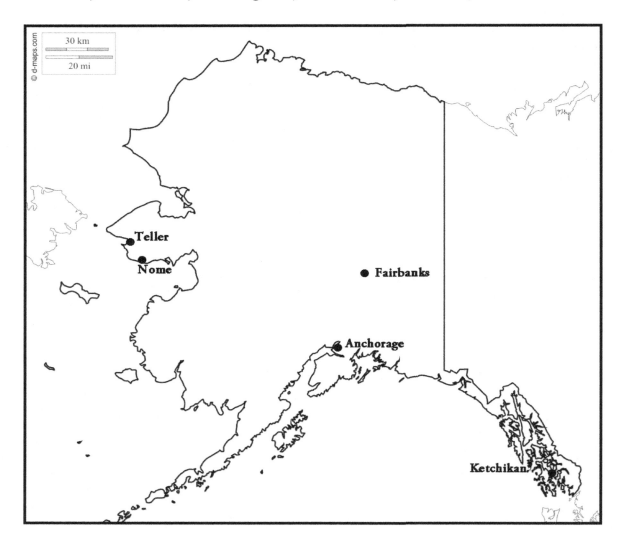

UNIT 7: EARLY ALASKA AVIATION

LESSON 23: CORDOVA FINALLY ENTERS AIR AGE

FACTS TO KNOW

Gorst Air Transport – Made plans to make the first trip across the Gulf of Alaska to Cordova

Gulf of Alaska – A broad inlet of the North Pacific on the south coast of Alaska

Clayton Scott – The first pilot to travel by airplane over the Gulf of Alaska to Cordova

COMPREHENSION QUESTIONS

1) When did aviation become important to Alaska? *Aviation became important to Alaska after the U.S. Army Black Wolf Squadron flyers flew to Nome in 1920. (Page 210)*

2) Why did it take so long for airplanes to come to Cordova? *The Gulf of Alaska frightened the boldest aerial navigators, and although aviators sometimes circled the town, none had ever landed. The area was notorious for bad weather that made it difficult to travel through. (Pages 209-210)*

3) How did the city of Cordova plan to celebrate the arrival of the Gorst Air Transport Company aircraft? *Harry O'Neil, president of the Chamber of Commerce, appointed a special committee. The committee planned a banquet, and the Cordova Tennis Club proposed entertaining the fliers, passengers and crew at the theater. The committee arranged for a huge welcome to sound when the planes were within sight. Whistles bellowing from the two fire engines, as well as every cannery and boat, would alert the residents that the planes had been spotted. (Pages 210-212)*

4) Explain why this historic event in Cordova didn't happen as scheduled.
Gorst Air Transport Company canceled its plans to land in Cordova after bad weather kicked up winds in May 1929. Clayton Scott offered to come to Cordova if four passengers could be secured. (Page 213)

5) What did pilot Clayon Scott say about Cordova and its residents after making the first aerial trip to the city? *In a speech, Scott said that the country between Cordova and Juneau was not a barrier, but ideal for flying. He declared that the town had shown not only that its location was ideal for an airport connecting interior and coastal cities, but that it had*

shown, in its spirit of friendliness, that the townspeople would aid in every way to have Cordova established as a leading air city of the North. (Pages 214, 217)

DISCUSSION QUESTION

(Discuss this question with your teacher or write your answer in essay form below. Use additional paper if necessary.)

Why do you think the residents of Cordova were so eager to have aircraft come to their city?

_____
_____
_____
_____
_____
_____
_____
_____
_____
_____
_____
_____
_____
_____
_____
_____
_____

LEARN MORE

Look for this book at your local library:
Alaska Aviation History, by Robert Stevens, 1990. Polynyas press, Des Moines, WA.

TIME TO REVIEW

Review Chapters 20-23 of your book before moving on the Unit Review. See how many questions you can answer without looking at your book.

Biplanes of the early 1900s took on many shapes, as seen in this photograph of Charles H. McNeil apparently sitting in one over Seattle.

UNIT 7: EARLY ALASKA AVIATION

REVIEW LESSONS 20-23

Write down what you remember about:

Henry Peterson – *He built Alaska's first airplane*

Arthur Williams – *Organized the first air show in Alaska with James Martin*

James V. Martin – *The first to fly in Alaska's skies*

Black Wolf Squadron – *Alaska flying expedition organized by Brig. Gen. William Mitchell*

Aviator – *A pilot, airman or airwoman*

Charles Otis Hammontree – *The first aviator to fly an amphibian aircraft in Anchorage*

Roy Franklin Jones – *Cook Inlet aviator who started a flying service in Ketchikan*

Merle Sasseen – *Well-known bush pilot*

Dirigible – *A lighter-than-air craft that is powered and steerable*

Norge – *Dirigible from Norway that traveled to the North Pole in 1926*

Roald Amundsen – *Famous explorer who traveled from Norway to Alaska in the Norge*

Gorst Air Transport – *Made plans to make the first trip across the Gulf of Alaska to Cordova*

Gulf of Alaska – *A broad inlet of the North Pacific on the south coast of Alaska*

Clayton Scott – *The first pilot to travel by airplane over the Gulf of Alaska to Cordova*

Fill in the blanks:

1) By 1911, flying events and air shows across the country were making news. And that's when _Nome_ resident _Henry Peterson_ decided to build Alaska's first _airplane_. The would-be pilot, who had no flying experience but had read much about _constructing and operating_ the plane, attempted lift off. But the machine did not _move/budge/fly._

2) _James V. Martin_ was the first to fly in Alaska's skies when promoter _Arthur Williams_ brought him north. The promoters thought they'd make a hefty profit with a Fourth of July _air show_.

3) Even though _Roy Franklin Jones_ found it too difficult to continue operating his flying service in _Ketchikan_ in the early 1920s, it wouldn't be long before _amphibious aircraft_ became one of the main modes of transportation in Southeast Alaska.

4) In the summer of 1923, _Anchorage_ resident _Arthur A. Shonbeck_ believed that his community needed to enter the air age. He organized and led the entire town in clearing a _field of trees, stumps and moss_ just beyond civilization for the town's first _airstrip_.

5) A typical aviator's outfit included two pairs of heavy wool _socks_, one pair of _caribou-skin_ socks, _moccasins_ that reached over the knees, heavy underwear, a pair of breeches, a pair of heavy trousers, a shirt and sweater, and a skin _cap and goggles_. The whole outfit then was covered with a knee-length _fur or skin parka_. Wool _gloves_ covered with heavy fur mitts protected their hands.

6) Famous explorer _Roald Amundsen_, who twice before had attempted to reach the _North Pole_ in conventional aircraft, realized his dream in the 348-foot airship called _Norge_ after he joined forces with a couple other men who were familiar with dirigibles.

7) _Nome_ residents were none too pleased when they learned that the huge craft – which had left _Norway_ to fly over the North Pole a few days earlier – had missed their beautiful town and landed in _Teller_ instead.

8) The first flight in Alaska soared in the skies of _Fairbanks_ in July _1913_. The _Black Wolf_ Squadron touched down in Wrangell, flew over Juneau and made its way to _Nome_ in 1920. Then a seaplane made its debut in the waters of _Cook Inlet_ near Anchorage in June 1922, and another flying boat landed in _Ketchikan_ a few weeks later. Even _Teller_ had seen a huge dirigible land on its shores in 1926. But by 1929, the city of _Cordova_ had yet to see its first aircraft landing.

9) _Gorst Air Transport_ Company canceled its plans to land in _Cordova_ after bad weather kicked up winds in May 1929. But the residents were cheered the next day when they received a report that one pilot, _Clayton Scott_, offered to fly to _Cordova_ if four passengers could be secured.

Early Alaska Aircraft
Word Scramble Key
Unscramble the words below

1.	toh ria onallbo	hot air balloon	Professor Leonard took one of these up into the air in Juneau in 1899
2.	nlapomoen	monoplane	A plane with one set of wings
3.	aplbien	biplane	A plane with multiple sets of wings
4.	De nHadlvial	De Havilland	The type of plane that came north with the Black Wolf Squadron
5.	apsealne	seaplane	Type of plane that can take off and land on water
6.	hanpiambi	amphibian	Another name for planes that can take off and land on water
7.	itrssuC yifgnl oabt	Curtiss flying boat	Pilot Roy Franklin Jones touched down in Ketchikan in one of these in 1922
8.	Hoiss nSrddtaa	Hisso Standard	This type of plane was the first to fly in Anchorage in 1924
9.	iiledgrib	dirigible	The Norge was one of these
10.	rracatfi	aircraft	Another name for planes

UNIT 7: EARLY ALASKA AVIATION

Unit Test

Choose *three* of the following questions to answer in paragraph form. Use as much detail as possible to completely answer the question.

1) Describe the first flight over Alaska. Who flew the plane? Where did he fly? How did Alaskans react to this historical event?

2) What are some of the ways air transportation impacted Alaska's history? Why was it so important to many Alaskans?

3) How did Roald Amundsen and his crew disappoint the residents of Nome in 1926? Explain what happened.

4) Why did it take so long for aviators to travel to Cordova? Who finally made the trip there? What did he say about Cordova after making the trip?

_____
_____
_____
_____
_____
_____
_____
_____
_____
_____
_____
_____
_____
_____
_____
_____
_____
_____
_____
_____
_____

TEACHER NOTES ABOUT THIS UNIT

TEACHER NOTES ABOUT THIS UNIT

Three members of the Black Wolf Squadron 1920 Alaska Air Expedition visit with young boy and his dog near a World War I bomber, an American De Havilland DH 4.

UNIT 8: DARING FLYBOYS

LESSON 24: EIELSON: ALASKA'S PIONEER AVIATOR

FACTS TO KNOW

Carl Benjamin Eielson – The pilot who flew the first commercial flight in Alaska
Commercial flight – For-profit flights to take passengers to a specific destination

COMPREHENSION QUESTIONS

1) Where was Carl Benjamin Eielson from? How did he end up in Alaska?
Carl Benjamin Eielson was born in 1897 in Hatton, North Dakota. While working as a guard at the capitol building in Washington D.C., he met Dan Sutherland, a former miner and Alaska's delegate to Congress, who persuaded Eielson to head to Alaska for a career as a schoolteacher. (Page 219)

2) What was the first commercial airplane company in Alaska? Who formed the company? _Carl Ben Eielson and a group of businessmen formed the Farthest-North Airplane Company in 1923. First National Bank of Fairbanks President Richard C. Wood and Fairbanks Daily News-Miner Editor William F. Thompson were named directors and Eielson became the sole pilot. (Page 220)_

3) Why did it take Carl Benjamin Eielson three times as long as it should have to get to Nenana ball field on his first flight there on July 4, 1923? _The pilot, plagued with a poor sense of direction, wandered around the skies for an hour and a half until he found the Nenana ball field and landed. (Page 220)_

4) Describe the first commercial flight in Alaska? How did this flight compare to the typical route from Fairbanks? _Eielson flew the first commercial flight in Alaska on July 16, 1923. Carrying attorney R.F. Roth and supplies, he landed at Denhart mines on Caribou Creek. Not only did it cost the Salchaket Mining Company $450 less for the plane ride compared to travel along the trail from Fairbanks, but it also saved time. The trail route took about six days, and the airplane trip took just a little more than an hour. (Page 222)_

5) How was Carl Benjamin Eielson involved in the start of airmail service in Alaska? _The U.S. government sent a De Havilland DH-4BM aircraft to Alaska for Carl Ben Eielson to use for experimental airmail runs between Nenana and McGrath. Eielson completed eight of 10 planned airmail runs – then a mishap caused substantial damage to the plane and ended any more flights with the De Havilland. (Pages 223-226)_

6) How did Carl Ben Eielson die at 32 years of age? *While attempting to rescue stranded passengers aboard the freight ship Nanuk, which was caught in the ice off the Siberian coast, Eielson and his mechanic, Earl Borland, ran into trouble. The wreckage of Eielsen's aircraft was located more than two months after it had been reported missing.* (Pages 228-229)

DISCUSSION QUESTION

(Discuss this question with your teacher or write your answer in essay form below. Use additional paper if necessary.)

Do you think that there are as many plane crashes today as there were in the early 1900s? Why or why not?

_____
_____
_____
_____
_____
_____
_____
_____
_____
_____
_____
_____
_____
_____
_____
_____

ENRICHMENT ACTIVITY

Look for this book at your local library:
Wings Over Alaska: The Story of Carl Ben Eielson, Edward A. Herron. New York: Julian Messner, 1959.

Write a one-page book report on what you learned about his life. What were the most interesting parts of the biography to you?

LEARN MORE

Read more about Carl Ben Eielson by visiting https://www.britannica.com/biography/Carl-Ben-Eielson

UNIT 8: DARING FLYBOYS

LESSON 25: WIEN: A LEGEND IN THE NORTH

FACTS TO KNOW

Noel Wien – Famous pilot who founded Wien Air Alaska in the 1930s
Ralph Wien – Older brother of Noel who became director of Fairbanks Airplane
  Corporation
"Anchorage" (not the city) – The plane that Noel Wien flew in Anchorage

COMPREHENSION QUESTIONS

1) Describe the scene that *Anchorage Daily Times* reported when Anchorage residents cleared land for their first airstrip. *"Men whose hands had not been soiled by anything heavier than a pen for many years, grappled the mattock or the axe and shook the kinks out of their flabby muscles. Ladies with rakes and other implements cleared away the small debris while others piled it upon the small mountain of stumps ready for the torch." (Page 232)*

2) What historic flight did Noel Wien fly on July 15, 1924? What needed to be done to prepare the plane for this flight? *James S. Rodebaugh hired Noel Wien to fly the first commercial flight between Anchorage and Fairbanks. Local mechanic Oscar Gill fabricated an auxiliary gas tank for the craft. It allowed the plane to travel several hundred miles without needing to refuel. (Pages 232-233)*

3) How did the historic flight referenced in Question #2 change the way that Alaskans thought about transportation? *Wien's first-ever flight between Anchorage and Fairbanks changed the way Alaskans thought about transportation forever. That same journey by train took two days. (Page 233)*

4) Name at least one other way that Noel Wien made history. *He was the first pilot to land above the Arctic Circle, made the first transcontinental flight between Alaska and Asia when he flew from Nome to Siberia, and completed the first commercial flight from Fairbanks to Seattle when he rushed pictures of the airplane crash that killed Will Rogers and pilot Wiley Post to the world in the 1930s. (Page 236)*

DISCUSSION QUESTION

(Discuss this question with your teacher or write your answer in essay form below. Use additional paper if necessary.)

How do you think modern life would be different without air travel?

_____
_____
_____
_____
_____
_____
_____
_____
_____
_____
_____
_____
_____
_____
_____
_____
_____
_____

ENRICHMENT ACTIVITY

You have learned a lot about the history of aviation in Alaska over the last two units of this course. Create your own timeline of Alaska aviation history beginning with Professor Leonard's first venture into Alaska's skies in 1899.

LEARN MORE

Look for this book at your local library:
The Wien Brothers' Story, by Kay Kennedy. Fairbanks Alaska, 1967.

UNIT 8: DARING FLYBOYS

LESSON 26: MERRILL: BLAZING TRAILS IN THE SKY

FACTS TO KNOW

Russell Hyde Merrill – The first pilot to fly a commercial flight across the Arctic Circle

Anchorage Air Transportation – Aviation company that Russell Merrill flew for in the 1920s

COMPREHENSION QUESTIONS

1) What was the first commercial flight westward from Juneau and the first attempt by a single-engine plane to cross the Gulf of Alaska? *Along with Roy Davis, Russell Merrill flew a Curtiss F Flying Boat to Seward in the first attempt by a single-engine plane to cross the Gulf of Alaska. It was the first commercial air flight westward from Juneau, as well. (Pages 239-240)*

2) Describe the flight that Russell Merrill and Noel Wien flew in 1928. How did Merrill almost die after the flight? *In May 1928, Russell Merrill flew with Noel Wien on the first commercial flights to Barrow for the Fox Film Expedition to Alaska to photograph Arctic scenes to be used later in a screen story. When they hit fog over the Colville River, they landed on a small ice-covered pond. Wien eventually took off with his pontooned plane, but Merrill could not fly off the pond. A dog musher later found Merrill snow blind, exhausted and unable to travel any farther on June 4. Merrill said after he'd eaten all the food he'd brought with him, he'd killed lemmings and eaten them raw. He almost died from Rocky Mountain spotted fever, caused by his diet of lemmings. (Pages 242-243)*

3) What happened to Russell Merrill? What are some theories? *On Sept. 16, 1929, Merrill took off alone in his float-equipped Travel Aire for Sleetemute and Bethel. No one ever saw him again. A piece of fabric was found on a Cook Inlet beach that was identified as coming from the tail section of Merrill's plane. Some believed he had fallen asleep and flown into the Inlet. Others thought he'd been forced down in the Inlet and had cut the fabric to use as a sail before the plane was swamped and sunk by the gale. (Pages 244-245)*

4) How did the city of Anchorage honor Russell Merrill? *Merrill had joined in petitioning for the establishment of a larger airfield for Anchorage before his death. In 1929, the land for Aviation Field was cleared. In June 1930, the new airfield was renamed Merrill Field. (Page 247)*

DISCUSSION QUESTION

(Discuss this question with your teacher or write your answer in essay form below. Use additional paper if necessary.)

What legacy did aviators like Russell Hyde Merrill, Carl Benjamin Eielson and Noel Wien leave?

_____
_____
_____
_____
_____
_____
_____
_____
_____
_____
_____
_____
_____
_____
_____
_____
_____

LEARN MORE

Read more about pioneer aviator Russell Hyde Merrill by visiting:
http://www.alaskahistory.org/biographies/merrill-russel-hyde/

TIME TO REVIEW

Review Chapters 24-26 of your book before moving on the Unit Review. See how many questions you can answer without looking at your book.

UNIT 7: DARING FLYBOYS

REVIEW LESSONS 24-26

Write down what you remember about:

Carl Benjamin Eielson – *The pilot who flew the first commercial flight in Alaska*

Commercial Flight – *For-profit flights to take passengers to a specific destination*

Noel Wien – *Famous pilot who founded Wien Air Alaska in the 1930s*

Ralph Wien – *Older brother of Noel who became director of Fairbanks Airplane Corporation*

"Anchorage" (not the city) – *The plane that Noel Wien flew in Anchorage*

Russell Hyde Merrill – *The first pilot to fly a commercial flight across the Arctic Circle*

Anchorage Air Transportation – *Aviation company that Russell Merrill flew for in the 1920s*

Fill in the blanks

1) *Carl Ben Eielson* made news on July 16, 1923, when he flew the first *commercial* flight in Alaska. Not only did it cost the *Salchaket Mining Company* $450 less for the plane ride compared to travel along the trail from *Fairbanks*, but it also saved time. The trail route took about six days, and the airplane trip took just *a little more than an hour.*

2) In 1924, the *U.S. government* sent a De Havilland DH-4BM aircraft to Alaska for pilot *Carl Ben Eielson* to use for experimental *airmail* runs between Nenana and McGrath.

3) James Rodebaugh hired *Noel Wien* to make the first-ever flight between *Anchorage* and *Fairbanks*. This historic flight, which lasted just under *five hours*, changed the way Alaskans thought about *transportation* forever. That same journey by *train* took two days.

4) To prepare for Noel Wien's historic flight, local mechanic Oscar Gill fabricated an auxiliary *gas tank* for the craft. It allowed the plane to travel several hundred miles without needing to *refuel*.

5) The summer of 1925 brought a milestone in Alaska aviation when two *mining operators* wanted to travel from *Fairbanks* to *Wiseman*. *Noel Wien* flew them to the village, located about 80 miles north of the *Arctic Circle*, thus making the first flight across the *Arctic*.

6) *Russell Merrill* made his first appearance in Alaska when he flew from *Portland, Oregon*, to *Juneau* in July 1925. In August, along with Roy Davis, he flew a Curtiss F Flying Boat to *Seward* in the first attempt by a single-engine plane to cross the *Gulf of Alaska*. It was the first *commercial* air flight westward from Juneau, as well.

7) In May 1928, *Russell Merrill* had one of his most narrow brushes with death. It was on the first commercial flight to *Barrow* for the Fox Film Expedition to Alaska to photograph *Arctic* scenes to be used later in a screen story. *Noel Wien* had the contract and needed another pilot.

8) A *dog musher* found *Russell Merrill* snow blind, exhausted and unable to travel any farther on June 4, 1928. *Merrill* said after he'd eaten all the food he'd brought with him, he'd killed *lemmings* and eaten them raw. He recovered from his blindness while in the Barrow hospital, but he almost died from *Rocky Mountain* spotted fever, caused by his diet of *lemmings*.

9) *Anchorage* city leaders approved a larger runway on the northern side of town, which later was named *Merrill Field* in honor of *Russell Hyde Merrill*.

UNIT 8: DARING FLYBOYS

Unit Test

Write at least three pragraphs about each of the three pioneer aviators that you studied in this unit. Be sure to include the following in your summation: What was this aviator most famous for? Describe one of his historic flights.

1) Carl Ben Eielson
2) Noel Wien
3) Russell Merrill

_____
_____
_____
_____
_____
_____
_____
_____
_____
_____
_____
_____
_____
_____
_____
_____
_____
_____
_____
_____
_____
_____
_____
_____
_____
_____
_____

TEACHER NOTES ABOUT THIS UNIT

TEACHER NOTES ABOUT THIS UNIT

Aviation Terms

Word Search Puzzle Key

Find the words listed below

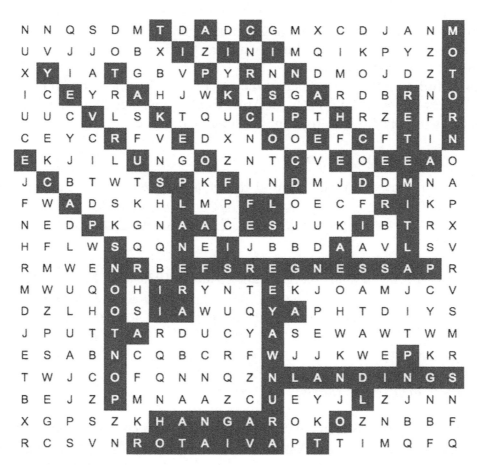

N	N	Q	S	D	M	T	D	A	D	C	G	M	X	C	D	J	A	N	M
U	V	J	J	O	B	X	I	Z	I	N	I	M	Q	I	K	P	Y	Z	O
X	Y	I	A	T	G	B	V	P	Y	R	N	N	D	M	O	J	D	Z	T
I	C	E	Y	R	A	H	J	W	K	L	S	G	A	R	D	B	R	N	O
U	U	C	V	L	S	K	T	Q	U	C	I	P	T	H	R	Z	E	F	R
C	E	Y	C	R	F	V	E	D	X	N	O	O	E	F	C	F	T	I	N
E	K	J	I	L	U	N	G	O	Z	N	T	C	V	E	O	E	E	A	O
J	C	B	T	W	T	S	P	K	F	I	N	D	M	J	D	D	M	N	A
F	W	A	D	S	K	H	L	M	P	F	L	O	E	C	F	R	I	K	P
N	E	D	P	K	G	N	A	A	C	E	S	J	U	K	I	B	T	R	X
H	F	L	W	S	Q	Q	N	E	I	J	B	B	D	A	A	V	L	S	V
R	M	W	E	N	R	B	E	F	S	R	E	G	N	E	S	S	A	P	R
M	W	U	Q	O	H	I	R	Y	N	T	E	K	J	O	A	M	J	C	V
D	Z	L	H	O	S	I	A	W	U	Q	Y	A	P	H	T	D	I	Y	S
J	P	U	T	T	A	R	D	U	C	Y	A	S	E	W	A	W	T	W	M
E	S	A	B	N	C	Q	B	C	R	F	W	J	J	K	W	E	P	K	R
T	W	J	C	O	F	Q	N	N	Q	Z	N	L	A	N	D	I	N	G	S
B	E	J	Z	P	M	N	A	A	Z	C	U	E	Y	J	L	Z	J	N	N
X	G	P	S	Z	K	H	A	N	G	A	R	O	K	O	Z	N	B	B	F
R	C	S	V	N	R	O	T	A	I	V	A	P	T	T	I	M	Q	F	Q

AVIATOR	AIRSPEED	ALTIMETER
AIRSPACE	AERIALSURVEY	COCKPIT
MOTOR	PLANE	HANGAR
AIRMAN	MECHANIC	AIRFIELD
PILOT	PONTOONS	PASSENGERS
TAKEOFFS	LANDINGS	RUNWAY

UNIT 9: FROM THE NEWSROOM 1930s

LESSON 27: NATIVES GAIN RECOGNITION

FACTS TO KNOW

Indian Reorganization Act of 1935 – U.S. law that allowed American Indians to locally govern their affairs by tribal government

William Lewis Paul Sr. – Tlingit man who was the first Alaska Native to serve in the Territorial Legislature in 1924

Bureau of Indian Affairs – Branch of the federal government that administers land held in trust by the United States for American Indians, including Alaska Natives, and also is responsible for providing for their health care

COMPREHENSION QUESTIONS

1) Why weren't Alaska Natives allowed to become citizens after America purchased Alaska in 1867? *Natives who continued to live traditional lifestyles were not considered "civilized" and therefore not recognized as U.S. citizens when America purchased Alaska from Russia in 1867. (Pages 248-249)*

2) What rights did the Indian Reorganization Act of 1935 afford Alaska Natives? (Be specific) *Amended in 1936 to include Alaska, the Indian Reorganization Act of 1935 allowed American Indians to locally govern their affairs by a tribal government that was established by constitution and bylaws for each tribe. Through its enactment, tribes were allowed to manage their own affairs, such as ownership and transfer of title to land and to keep records of vital events, establish their own police and court systems and set the terms of enrollment in their tribes. (Pages 248-249)*

3) When were Alaska Natives given the right to vote? What conditions had to be met? *It took years of hard work, but Alaska Natives were given the right to vote in 1922. However, certain conditions had to be met. "Wear Western clothing; not eat Indian foods or speak Indian languages; and live apart from Indian village communities" were among the list of criteria that would make an Alaska Native eligible to vote. (Page 250)*

4) What two milestones occurred in Alaska Native history in 1924? *A milestone was passed in 1924 when Congress extended citizenship to all Indians in the United States and Tlingit William L. Paul Sr. was elected as the first Native to the Alaska Territorial Legislature. (Pages 251-252)*

5) Describe the educational system for Native Alaskan children in the early 1900s.
In 1928, a court case resolved the right of Native children to attend public school. The "civilized persons" mentality in the territory persevered, however. Native children were instructed to speak only English. And those who attended Bureau of Indian Affairs schools in their own villages often were forcibly sent to BIA boarding schools elsewhere if they were caught speaking their indigenous language. (Page 254)

DISCUSSION QUESTION

(Discuss this question with your teacher or write your answer in essay form below. Use additional paper if necessary.)

What do you think about the requirements placed upon Alaska Natives to dress in "western clothing" and speak only English?

_____
_____
_____
_____
_____
_____
_____
_____
_____
_____
_____
_____
_____
_____
_____
_____

ENRICHMENT ACTIVITY

Read the article at this link http://www.akhistorycourse.org/alaskas-cultures/tribal-governments-federal-law and then write a one-page summary about what you learned.

LEARN MORE

Tlingit Stories, by Maria Ackerman. Anchorage: Alaska Methodist University, 1975.

Read more about the Indian Reorganization Act and other important milestones in Alaska Native history by visiting http://www.akhistorycourse.org/governing-alaska/native-citizenship-and-land-issues

UNIT 9: FROM THE NEWSROOM 1930s

LESSON 28: COLONISTS SETTLE VALLEY

FACTS TO KNOW

Matanuska Valley – Area of southcentral Alaska known for agriculture

Col. Otto F. Ohlson – General Manager of the Alaska Railroad who helped start the Matanuska Valley Colony project

Great Depression of 1930s – The largest worldwide economic depression of the 20th century

The New Deal – A series of programs enacted by U.S. President Franklin D. Roosevelt to boost the economy between 1933-1939

COMPREHENSION QUESTIONS

1) Long before the _Matanuska Valley_ in _Southcentral_ Alaska became one of the fastest-growing regions in the nation, _Russians_ experimented in its fertile soil. They taught the _Tanaina/Dena'ina_ to grow crops like _potatoes, carrots, rasishes and turnips. (Page 258)_

2) Why was the Matanuska Valley a good area for farming?
The area had fertile soil and abundant sources of fresh water. (Page 258)

3) How did the Great Depression of the 1930s jump-start the population growth of the Matanska Valley? _In an effort to take people away from rural districts, where poverty had prevailed long before the Depression, and move them into areas where they might lead more productive lives, U.S. President Franklin D. Roosevelt's administration designed many resettlement projects. Roosevelt approved the project known as the Matanuska Valley Colony in his New Deal in 1935. (Pages 258-260)_

4) When colonists arrived in Alaska as part of the Matanuska Valley Colony project, what did they receive? _The farmers drew lots for 40 acres and a homestead, a deal that included a house, barn, outbuildings, a well and livestock. They also received loans for $3,000 at 3 percent interest to pay for it all. In addition, each family was given temporary housing, a food allowance of $75, medical care and help clearing the land and building a home._ (Page 266)

5) What was life like for the colonists? *With a short growing season upon them, the colonists immediately went to work tilling and planting while temporarily living in tents. Some colonists also bitterly complained that officials were taking too long to build their homes and barns and that conditions at the colony were less than ideal. Others worked diligently to adapt.* (Pages 265-278)

DISCUSSION QUESTION

(Discuss this question with your teacher or write your answer in essay form below. Use additional paper if necessary.)

How did Alaskans feel about the colonists who arrived in Alaska under the Matanuska Valley Colony project?

_____
_____
_____
_____
_____
_____
_____
_____
_____
_____
_____
_____
_____
_____
_____

ENRICHMENT ACTIVITY

Imagine that you are one of the colonists who relocated to the Matanuska Valley. Write a letter to a friend or family member about your adventures traveling to Alaska and settling in the valley.

LEARN MORE

Read more about farming history in Alaska by visiting http://www.akhistorycourse.org/americas-territory/alaskas-heritage/chapter-4-17-farming-herding-and-lumbering

UNIT 9: FROM THE NEWSROOM 1930s

LESSON 29: SOURDOUGH GOVERNOR APPOINTED

FACTS TO KNOW

John Weir Troy – Served as Alaska's 12th territorial governor from 1933-1939
University of Alaska – The first university in Alaska and was established at Fairbanks

COMPREHENSION QUESTIONS

1) Why did Alaskans heave a collective sigh of relief when John Troy was appointed the territory's 12th governor? *Troy knew Alaska and knew what to do to make it stronger. He'd mined, mushed, trapped and fished with the masses. He'd been rich and poor, and he'd lived through hardships and knew about luxury. Gov. "Johnny" was a true Alaskan through and through. Oldtimers believed that he knew what it took to get Alaska statehood. (Page 282)*

2) What led John Troy to Alaska in 1897? What did he do for work when he got there? *The gold rush led him to set sail for Skagway in 1897 on a boat carrying "other mules and some horses." He didn't find nuggets, but instead found work hauling gold seekers from Skagway over the mountains and waterways into Whitehorse. After the gold fever subsided, he became editor of the Skagway Daily Alaskan. When it folded, he moved to Juneau and became editor of the Daily Alaska Empire, which he soon purchased and ran for 27 years. (Page 281)*

3) What did John Troy believe was Alaska's greatest need? What did he think was needed in order to accomplish this? *John Troy believed that more people was Alaska's greatest need. He was a firm believer that the territory should become a state. And Troy thought a larger population and a better road system would help achieve that goal. (Pages 281-282)*

4) How was John Troy involved in boosting centers of learning in the territory? *In 1935, he signed the law that changed the name of the college in Fairbanks and started the illustrious University of Alaska. The institution officially began in 1917 as a college, but its origins lie in the creation in 1906 of a federal agricultural experiment station in Fairbanks, the sixth in Alaska. The station set the stage for the university that developed later, which is strongly research-oriented. (Page 284)*

DISCUSSION QUESTION

(Discuss this question with your teacher or write your answer in essay form below. Use additional paper if necessary.)

What did John Troy think about the Matanuska Valley Colony project?

_____
_____
_____
_____
_____
_____
_____
_____
_____
_____
_____
_____
_____
_____
_____
_____
_____

ENRICHMENT ACTIVITY

Watch this short YouTube video to learn more about the New Deal:
https://www.youtube.com/watch?v=U_FVa_Rx_ek

LEARN MORE

Read more about John Wier Troy by visiting http://www.juneau.org/library/museum/
GCM/readarticle.php?UID=797&newxtkey=

UNIT 9: FROM THE NEWSROOM 1930s

LESSON 30: BLACK FOG OVER BARROW

FACTS TO KNOW

Will Rogers – Beloved humorist who died in a plane crash near Point Barrow in 1935
Wiley Post – The pilot of the plane who died along with Will Rogers when they crashed in 1935
Barrow – The farthest-north community in the United States near the area that Wiley Post and Will Rogers crashed and died; in 2016, the community voted for the town to retake its original name of Utqiaġvik

COMPREHENSION QUESTIONS

1) Why did Wiley Post want to fly to Alaska? Why did Will Rogers want to fly to Alaska?
Post had been to Alaska before and wanted to go back and see if it would be feasible to lay out a mail and passenger route between Alaska and Russia to avoid the long Pacific flight. Listening to Post fired up Will Rogers' imagination and revived his desire to see Alaska for the first time. (Page 288)

2) What was Rogers' and Post's intended destination for the trip?
Post's and Rogers' plans were vague when they took off from Seattle early in August 1935 for the "Roof of the World," Point Barrow. They had no particular destination and planned to make it a vacation trip by easy stages. Rogers was paying the expenses, and they had half-formed plans of flying around the world by way of Siberia, China, Ethiopia, Europe and Greenland. (Page 290)

3) What warnings did the men receive about the flight to Barrow?
Rex Beach said it sounded decidedly risky. He tried to discourage Rogers from flying to Point Barrow. Stanley Morgan, in charge of the weather station there, warned that the fog was impossible, but Post finally made the decision. "I think I can make it," he said. And Rogers replied: "If it's good enough for you, it's good enough for me." (Pages 290-295)

4) Why did Post land in the water 12 miles away from Barrow? What did he and Rogers do when they landed there? *After clearing through the mountains, they eventually got lost in the fog. When they spotted a lone figure standing by a camp near a lagoon, Post brought the plane down and landed on the water. The pair then waded ashore and asked the man, an Eskimo named Claire Okpeha, how far they were from Barrow. (Pages 295-296)*

5) What happened when Wiley Post and Will Rogers took off after landing on the water 12 miles from Barrow? _On learning Barrow was only 12 miles away, the adventurers returned to the plane and took off. According to Okpeha, everything seemed to go all right until they were up about 400 or 500 feet. Then suddenly their engine sputtered and died. As Okpeha watched, the plane went into a nose dive, hitting the shallow lagoon with the speed of a rocket and turning completely over so that engine and fuselage were buried under three feet of water. Both men were killed in the crash._ (Page 296)

DISCUSSION QUESTION

(Discuss this question with your teacher or write your answer in essay form below. Use additional paper if necessary.)

How was Will Rogers remembered after his death? What are some ways that he was honored after his death?

_____
_____
_____
_____
_____
_____
_____
_____
_____
_____
_____
_____
_____
_____
_____
_____
_____
_____

LEARN MORE

Read more about Will Rogers by visiting http://www.willrogers.com/the-man

MAP ACTIVITY

Find the following places on the map where Will Rogers and Wiley Post traveled:
1) Juneau   2) Anchorage   3)Matanuska Valley   4) Fairbanks   5) Barrow

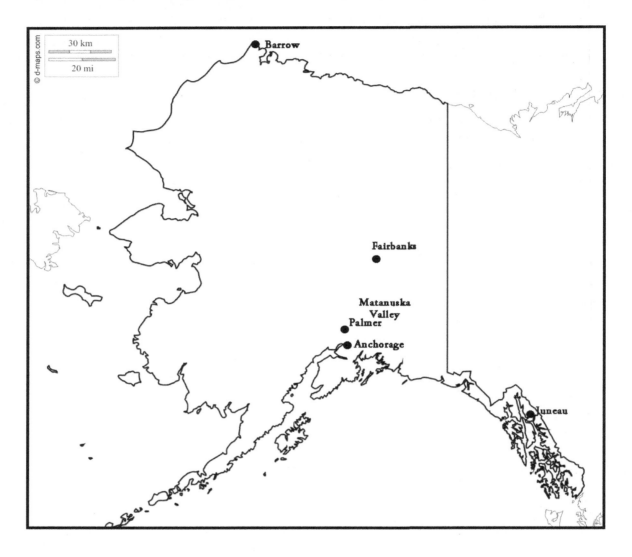

After getting lost in a fog, Wiley Post finally saw a lone reindeer herder, like this man, near a lagoon so he landed his plane to ask for directions to Barrow.

UNIT 9: FROM THE NEWSROOM 1930s

LESSON 31: OTHER NEWS AROUND ALASKA

Write 1-2 brief sentences summarizing each headline:

1) **Anchorage 1935 – First Fur Rendezvous Celebrated**
The first annual Fur Rendezvous included a fur swap meet, blanket toss, parade and three-day sporting events. (Page 303)

2) **Bristol Bay 1935 – Salmon was King**
Salmon packs peaked at 8,437,603 cases in 1935, and Fortune magazine published a long report on Pacific Ocean fish that found Alaska's canned salmon shipments were worth more than all the state's gold, silver, copper, furs and other fish combined. (Page 304)

3) **Fairbanks 1935 – Ice Carnival Created**
The Fairbanks Ice Carnival featured an ice carnival queen, decked out in a fur-trimmed parka and mukluks. The newly formed University of Alaska Polar Bear hockey team took on the Dawson, Yukon Territory team. (Page 305)

4) **Juneau 1935 – Labor Strike Ends in Violence**
On May 22, 1935, 900 Alaska-Juneau Gold Mine Company workers walked off the job to protest wages and working conditions. Violence broke out after a new miners association, backed by the company, formed and marched to the A-J employment office on June 24. (Page 306)

5) **Ketchikan 1935 – Alaska Sportsman Born**
In 1935, Emery Tobin and several others – including popular local artist Bill Gabler and well-known resident Ray Roady – formed a corporation to publish a magazine that focused on stories about hunting, fishing and adventure in Alaska, plus editorials that addressed Alaska's political challenges. That publication today is known as the Alaska Magazine. (Page 308)

6) **Nome 1934 – Fire Destroys Downtown Businesses**
Fire swept through Nome in 1934 and wiped out most of the downtown area – much like the fire that destroyed Nome's business district in 1905. Residents had rebuilt much of the downtown area by 1937. (Page 309)

7) Palmer 1936 – First Fair in the Valley

The first Palmer Fair in 1936 was held on school grounds. The event coincided with the opening of the Knik River Bridge, which linked Anchorage and the Valley by road for the first time. *(Page 310)*

8) Valdez 1932 – Aviator Reeve Arrived in Alaska

In January 1932, aviator Robert Reeve stowed away in the chain locker of a steamship and landed in Alaska with $2 in his pocket. Within a couple of years, he'd built this hangar in Valdez and was starting to make a name for himself in Alaska aviation. *(Page 311)*

LEARN MORE

Look for this book at your local library:
The Alaskans, by Wheeler, Keith. Alexandria, Virginia: Time-Life Books, 1977.

TIME TO REVIEW

Review Chapters 27-31 of your book before moving on the Unit Review. See how many questions you can answer without looking at your book.

UNIT 9: FROM THE NEWSROOM 1930s

REVIEW LESSONS 27-31

Write down what you remember about:

Reorganization Act of 1935 – *U.S. law that allowed American Indians to locally govern their affairs by tribal government*

William Lewis Paul Sr. – *Tlingit man who was the first Alaska Native to serve in the Territorial Legislature in 1924*

Bureau of Indian Affairs – *Branch of the federal government that administers land held in trust by the U.S. for American Indians, including Alaska Natives, and also is responsible for providing for their health care*

Matanuska Valley – *Area of Southcentral Alaska known for agriculture*

Col. Otto F. Ohlson – *General Manager of the Alaska Railroad who helped start the Matanuska Valley Colony project*

Great Depression of 1930s – *The largest worldwide economic depression of the 20th century*

The New Deal – *A series of programs enacted by U.S. President Franklin D. Roosevelt to boost the economy between 1933-1939*

John Weir Troy – *Served as Alaska's 12th territorial governor from 1933-1939*

University of Alaska – *The first university in Alaska and was established at Fairbanks*

Will Rogers – *Beloved humorist who died in a plane crash near Point Barrow in 1935*

Wiley Post – *The pilot of the plane who died along with Will Rogers when they crashed in 1935*

Barrow – *The farthest-north community in the United States near the area that Wiley Post and Will Rogers crashed and died; in 2016, the community voted for the town to retake its original name of Utqiaġvik*

Fill in the blanks:

1) Amended in *1936* to include Alaska, the *Indian Reorganization Act of 1935* allowed American Indians to locally govern their affairs by a *tribal* government that was established by constitution and bylaws for each tribe.

2) It took years of hard work, but Alaska Natives were given the right to *vote* in 1922. However, certain *conditions* had to be met such as: wear *Western clothing*; not *eat Native/Indian foods* or speak *Native/Indian languages*; and live apart from *Native/Indian village communities*.

3) *Col. Otto F. Ohlson*, general manager of the Alaska Railroad since 1928, also had been trying to entice *farmers* to the *Matanuska Valley* in an effort to spur railbelt settlement toward Palmer. But despite the area's *fertile* valleys and abundant sources of fresh water, settlers didn't stream into the area.

4) *Col. Otto F. Ohlson* helped the Department of Interior and the Federal Emergency Rehabilitation Administration plan a *farming* community, and U.S. President *Franklin D. Roosevelt* approved the project known as the *Matanuska Valley* Colony in his New Deal in 1935.

5) The *farmers/colonists* under the *Matanuska Valley* Colony project drew lots for 40 acres and a homestead, a deal that included a *house, barn, outbuildings, a well and livestock*. They also received *loans* for *$3,000* at 3 percent interest to pay for it all. In addition, each family was given temporary *housing*, a *food* allowance of $75, medical care and help clearing the land and building a *home*.

6) *John Weir Troy* served as Alaska's 12th territorial governor from 1933-1939. He was a firm believer that the territory should become a *state*. And Troy thought a larger *population* and a better *road* system would help achieve that goal.

7) *John Weir Troy* also believed in boosting centers of *learning* in the territory. In 1935, he signed the *law* that changed the name of the college in Fairbanks and started the illustrious *University of Alaska*.

8) *Flora Jane Harper* of *Rampart* became the first Alaska Native to graduate from the *University of Alaska* in Fairbanks in 1935.

9) Aviator *Wiley Post* invited humorist *Will Rogers* to travel to Alaska and beyond with him in 1935. Their plans were vague when they took off from Seattle early in August for the "Roof of the World," *Point Barrow.*

10) On learning that *Barrow* was only 12 miles away, the adventurers returned to the plane and took off. According to an Eskimo named *Claire Okpeha*, everything seemed to go all right until they were up about 400 or 500 feet. Then suddenly their *engine sputtered and died*. The plane went into a *nose dive*, hitting the shallow lagoon with the speed of a rocket and *turned completely over* so that engine and fuselage were buried under three feet of water.

Greetings from Fairbanks, Alaska

Season's Best Wishes

This postcard illustrates the talent of ice carvers in Fairbanks, home of the Ice Carnival.

From the Newsroom 1930s

Crossword Puzzle

Read Across and Down clues and fill in blank boxes that match numbers on the clues

Across

4 Town that sometimes is called "the top of the world"
9 Last name of reindeer herder who gave men directions before fatal crash in 1935
10 The new Southcentral farmers' community received 18 miles of netting to battle this pest in 1935
11 Name of steamship that carried first group of farmers to Alaska in 1935
12 Aviation pioneer who crashed and died near "the top of the world" in 1935
13 Alaska governor from 1933-1939
15 Alaska Natives were not considered this when Alaska became part of the United States in 1867
18 Government minted tokens that farmers used as currency in 1935
19 This swept through Nome in 1934, and Seward in 1935, and destroyed most of their downtown areas
23 Name for an old-timer in Alaska
25 A procession of people or vehicles moving through a public place
28 Will Rogers' hometown in Oklahoma
30 Name of pilot who carried two bodies from "the top of the world" back to the States
32 This arrived in the Southcentral Alaska farmers' community long before farmers could use it in 1935
34 Rex Beach said that Alaska summer weather can be this
36 Sometimes called "farmers of the sea"
37 The people who taught Alaska Natives to grow crops in the 1800s
38 What the farmers who came to Southcentral Alaska in 1935 were called
39 Reason airplane got lost heading to "the top of the world" in 1935
40 An institution of higher learning
41 Valley where farmers from Midwestern and Northern states settled in 1935 to begin farming
42 Alaska Natives were given the right to do this (under certain conditions) in 1922
43 Structures farmers first lived in when they arrived to build an agricultural community in 1935

Down

1 Type of body of water that Rogers' plane crashed into before fatal 1935 crash
2 Much-loved humorist who traveled to Alaska in 1935 and then died in an airplane crash
3 The U.S. government sent 150 horses to the new Southcentral Alaska farmers' community but forgot to send any of these in 1935
5 Game played at the first Ice Carnival in Fairbanks
6 Renewable resource that was king in the 1930s
7 A person's or family's residence, which comprises the land, house and outbuildings
8 Name of schooner that stalled on a sandbar near Ugashik Bay in 1935
13 Alaska Natives were given authority to have this type of government under the Indian Reorganization Act of 1935
14 First Alaska Native to graduate from the University of Alaska Fairbanks in 1935
16 Reason that first group of farmers were quarantined on the steamship for a week when they arrived in Seward in April 1935
17 Aviator who arrived in Valdez in 1932 and later built one of Alaska's best-known airways
20 Southeast town where labor unrest occurred in May 1935

From the Newsroom 1930s
Crossword Puzzle Key

Down (Continued)

21 Town in Matanuska Valley where the first fair was held in 1936
22 Tough economic times are called this
24 Name of celebration that began in Anchorage in 1935 that centered around furs
26 Some, including governor during 1933-1939, thought more of this would help Alaska become a state
27 Woman crowned this at Fairbanks Ice Festival
29 U.S. President who created the New Deal programs during the 1930s
31 Name of publication born in 1935 that later became known as the *Alaska Magazine*
33 William Lewis Paul Sr., the first Alaska Native to serve in Alaska's Territorial Legislature, belonged to this Native group
35 He was general manager of the Alaska Railroad and tried to get farmers interested in agriculture during the late 1920s-early 1930s

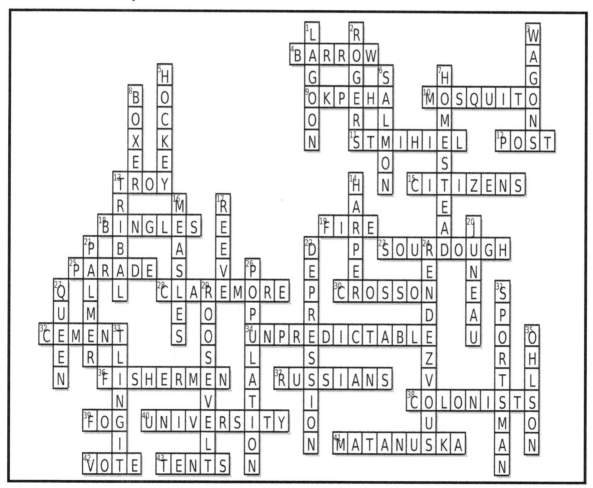

UNIT 9: FROM THE NEWSROOM 1930s

Unit Test

Choose *three* of the following questions to answer in paragraph form. Use as much detail as possible to completely answer the question.

1) Why weren't Alaska Natives considered citizens when the United States purchased Alaska in 1867? What kind of requirements did Alaska Natives need to meet in order to vote in 1922?

2) What was the purpose of the Matanuska Valley Colony project? How did it benefit the colonists? How did it benefit Alaska?

3) Name two major things that John Weir Troy accomplished while serving as Alaska's 12th territorial governor from 1933-1939.

4) Describe what happened when Wiley Post and Will Rogers took a trip to Alaska.